New Zealand

New Zealand

BY DONNA WALSH SHEPHERD

Enchantment of the World
Second Series

Children's Press®

A Division of Scholastic Inc.

NEW YORK   TORONTO   LONDON   AUCKLAND   SYDNEY
MEXICO CITY   NEW DELHI   HONG KONG
DANBURY, CONNECTICUT

Frontispiece: Crossing the Fox River in Paparoa National Park

Consultant: Dr. Russell Kirkpatrick, lecturer, Department of Geography, University of Waikato. Author: *Contemporary Atlas of New Zealand* and deputy editor *Historical Atlas of New Zealand.*

Please note: *All statistics are as up-to-date as possible at the time of publication.*

Book production by Herman Adler Design

Library of Congress Cataloging-in-Publication Data

Walsh Shepherd, Donna
    New Zealand / by Donna Walsh Shepherd
      p. cm. — (Enchantment of the world. Second series)
    Includes bibliographical references and index.
    ISBN 0-516-21099-8
    1. New Zealand—Juvenile literature. [1. New Zealand.] I. Title. II. Series.
DU408 .W35 2002
993—dc21   00-065957

Acknowledgments

First and foremost, I want to thank the many kind people of New Zealand who so generously shared their time and their stories with me. I especially want to thank Lynley Twyman of the Canterbury Tourism Bureau who spent much time with me on her day off pointing me in all the right directions. And thank you to the good people of the Te Papa Museum, a truly amazing place. And to the young Maori woman who gave me much information and shared the breath of life with me so that this book may more fully tell the Maori story. And to Jock Phillips, New Zealand's chief historian, and the Department of Conservation for their insight and information. And to Leonardo's in Queenstown for making such good cappuccinos on such cold rainy days.

And thank you to my family who traveled the roads of my research with me. All brought their own interests to broaden my research. My husband, Morris Shepherd, captained the van so expertly across the country on the left side of the road. My sons, Chad, Shane, and Aaron Shepherd, changed their schedules so we could have yet one more "last family trip," then took us climbing mountains, bungeeing off cliffs, sampling wines, and listening to symphonies and pub music. My parents, Maurice and Bernice Walsh, brought their birding skills, art knowledge, and patience. And, of course, thanks to Jimmy, whose unfailing good humor got us up and kept us going each day.

This book is dedicated to the Traveling Team: Maurice and Bernice Walsh; Morris and Donna Shepherd; Chad, Shane, and Aaron Shepherd. May all journeys be so joyful.

Contents

Cover photo:
Child playing
in pasture

CHAPTER

ONE   The Land of the Long White Cloud 8

TWO   Where Two Plates Meet 14

THREE   An Island of Birds 30

FOUR   From Wilderness to Commonwealth 42

FIVE   Two Queens and a Parliament 62

SIX   Growing a Good Living 74

SEVEN   Thumbprints of the People 88

EIGHT   Living in the Godzone 96

NINE   The Art of Kiwi Fun 102

TEN   Growing Up Kiwi 116

Church on Lake Tekapo

Timeline.....................**128**

Fast Facts..................**130**

To Find Out More...........**134**

Index......................**136**

Maori festival

The Land of the Long White Cloud

ON THE SOUTH ISLAND OF NEW ZEALAND, LUSH FORESTS climb the steep mountain walls and crowd into the river valleys. The December summer sun turns the trees rich shades of green. Nesting birds call back and forth. Sheep graze in high pastures just above the vineyards where grapes ripen on gentle slopes. Beyond the mountain ridge, the ocean kisses the rocky shore, while little blue penguins swim out to sea to feast on fish. It is so beautiful, so serene here, surely this valley is the birthplace of peace and contentment.

Then the serenity is pierced by a scream plunging down, echoing off the mountain cliffs and into the river valley. The scream vanquishes the peace and jars the birds. They fly out of the trees past a falling body. The scream continues and the body falls faster toward the river rushing through the deep gorge.

But no worries, mate. This is New Zealand. That scream is the sound of delight and adventure. That scream is the scream of a bungee jumper, arms flailing in the air, plunging off a bridge and into New Zealand's reputation for fun. In this peaceful river valley bungee jumping was invented. Here beauty and the bizarre go hand in hand. Here there are "no worries, mate" and everything fun is "pure NZ."

An Exclamation Point of Islands

On the map some think New Zealand looks like a broken exclamation point. Two long islands, North Island and South

Opposite: **Clouds over Milford Sound**

Bungee jumping was invented in New Zealand.

Geopolitical map of
New Zealand

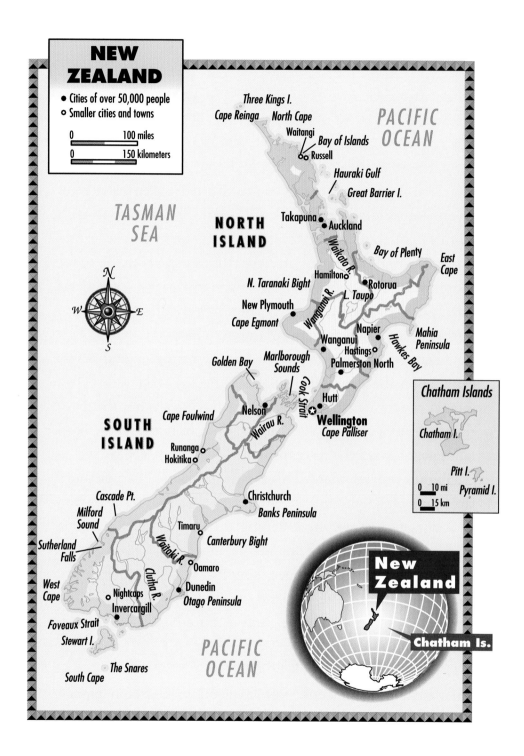

NEW ZEALAND

- Cities of over 50,000 people
- Smaller cities and towns

0   100 miles
0   150 kilometers

PACIFIC OCEAN

Three Kings I.
Cape Reinga
North Cape
Waitangi
Bay of Islands
Russell

Hauraki Gulf
Great Barrier I.

TASMAN SEA

NORTH ISLAND

Takapuna
Auckland

Waikato R.

Bay of Plenty
East Cape

Hamilton
Rotorua
L. Taupo

N. Taranaki Bight

New Plymouth
Cape Egmont

Wanganui R.

Napier
Mahia Peninsula

Wanganui
Hastings
Hawkes Bay

Palmerston North

Golden Bay

Marlborough Sounds

Cook Strait

Nelson

Cape Foulwind

Wairau R.

Hutt
Wellington
Cape Palliser

SOUTH ISLAND

Runanga
Hokitika

Cascade Pt.
Milford Sound
Sutherland Falls

Christchurch
Banks Peninsula

Timaru

Canterbury Bight

Waitaki R.

Oamaru

Clutha R.

Dunedin
Otago Peninsula

West Cape

Nightcaps
Invercargill

Foveaux Strait
Stewart I.

The Snares
South Cape

PACIFIC OCEAN

Chatham Islands

Chatham I.

Pitt I.
Pyramid I.

0   10 mi
0   15 km

New Zealand

Chatham Is.

Island, form the body, and Stewart Island is the dot at the end of the excitement. It is appropriate that of all countries, it's New Zealand that reminds us of an exclamation point. New Zealand deserves plenty of !!!'s for its beauty, its uniqueness, its social and economic successes, and its devotion to any challenging sport.

Even the history of New Zealand is filled with adventure. A thousand years ago the islands were quiet and peaceful, inhabited mostly by birds. Legends tell us that somewhere between 1,500 and 800 years ago, Polynesian adventurers living north of the equator set out exploring in outrigger canoes. They sailed farther south than they ever had previously. Finally one day, low on the horizon, they saw a long white cloud. Kupe, the leader and a great navigator, knew the cloud was likely caught on the mountains of a distant land. He named the land *Aotearoa*, Land of the Long White Cloud.

At Aotearoa they found a beautiful green land of mountains, plains, rivers, and lakes. Sealife filled the waters offshore. Giant birds, providing eggs and meat, filled the forests. A few hundred years later, the Maori, descendants of those early explorers, made a permanent home there. These islands were nearly the last major landmass to be settled by people. Only Antarctica was later.

Maori in a traditional canoe greet a replica of the *Endeavour*, the ship Captain Cook sailed to New Zealand.

Eventually European explorers also found Aotearoa. Dutch, British, and French explorers all came. The Dutch called the new land *Nieuw Zeeland*, after the Zeeland province in the Netherlands.

Sealers and whalers, missionaries, and settlers from many countries followed the explorers. Through battles and treaties, the islands became the nation of New Zealand and a member of the British Commonwealth. The Maori lost their right to self-rule, but today they are reclaiming their culture and some of their land rights. Aotearoa has become a bicultural society.

Kiwi Spirit

New Zealanders of all heritages are affectionately called Kiwis after the national bird—an oddly charming, round, fuzzy brown bird that can't fly. The bird has become a symbol of the uniqueness of New Zealand and its people.

Kiwis describe their country proudly as clean and green. New Zealand is among the cleanest countries in the world. A population of under 4 million in an area the size of Japan has helped moderate the impact of people on the environment. Graffiti and litter are rare. Gardens and public art are plentiful. Subtropical rain and sun provide a good climate for abundant plantlife, both natural and cultivated. Most people have a bit of land for a garden and flowers. Ellerslie, the

The kiwi is New Zealand's national bird.

largest garden show in the Southern Hemisphere, takes place in Auckland each spring in November.

New Zealanders also work at cultivating a "green attitude." In its early history, New Zealand's forests were quickly cut for timber or burned to create pastureland. Many animals became endangered or went extinct. In recent years, New Zealanders have made a strong commitment toward

Flowers grace a village cottage

the preservation and protection of their environment. They are fighting decades of erosion with replantings, working on protecting threatened species, and have declared their country a nuclear-free zone.

Today, New Zealand's economy thrives mostly on trade, farming and industries that support farming, and tourism. As the demand for wool has declined, New Zealanders have turned to new products and crops, especially dairy, lumber, and agricultural exports. They are pursuing international tourism as a source of high-income, low-impact revenue. Today people from all over the world come to New Zealand for the natural beauty and outdoor recreation. But many just want to be strapped onto that bundle of bungee rubber bands and jump off bridges and cliffs. The Kiwis just smile at their good fortune, pocket the money, and say, "See you at the bottom, mate." And a new body gets ready to take that plunge into the gorge.

Where Two Plates Meet

THE ANCIENT POLYNESIAN VOYAGERS BELIEVED MAUI, THEIR god of fire, created the mountainous islands of New Zealand by pulling them up from the bottom of the ocean. Just as the ancients believed, much of New Zealand's land did come from below the ocean. New Zealand is anchored on the Ring of Fire—the string of volcanoes that circles the north and south Pacific Ocean.

New Zealand sits atop the line where the Pacific plate meets the Indo-Australian Plate. Far underwater these two bodies of land slide against each other. Where the Pacific plate folds under the Australian plate, volcanoes gush to the surface. These volcanoes have created much of the North Island.

Although both islands are long and narrow, the South Island has quite different geography. Under the South Island the plates push against each other instead of folding into one another. The continual pushing over many millennia causes the surface land to smash abruptly upward. This creates sharply jagged mountains, such as the Southern Alps. These mountains are

Opposite: **A North Island beach**

South Island rock formations called the Pancake Rocks

A geothermal mud pool on North Island

still growing at about two-fifths of an inch (10 millimeters) a year. As the land pushes up, it also spreads out. Christchurch on the East Coast is moving away from Hokitika on the West Coast at the rate of an inch (25 mm) a year. Just like the mountains and valleys of the South Island, the ocean floor around the islands is deeply trenched and ridged.

No place on earth has so much geographical variety packed into such a small area. New Zealand is only about the size of California, England, or Japan. But it has sun-drenched subtropical beaches, a string of volcanoes, geothermal mudpools and geysers, orchards and pastures, glacier-topped mountains, rain forests, grassland plains, deep ancient forests, steep-sided fjords, and rocky, windswept, desolate islands. Maui seems to have blessed New Zealand with everything except deserts.

Geographical Features

Area: 104,454 square miles (270,534 sq km)

Highest Elevation: Mount Cook, 12,349 feet (3,764 m) above sea level

Highest Volcano: Ruapehu 9,175 feet (2,797 m)

Lowest Elevation: Sea level along the coast

Longest River: Waikato River, 264 miles (425 km) long

Highest Waterfall: Sutherland Falls, 1,904 feet (580 m) high; the world's fifth-largest waterfall

Largest Park: Fjordland, 3.2 million acres (1.3 million ha)

Largest Lake: Lake Taupo, 234 square miles (606 sq km)

Coastline: 3,200 miles (5,150 km)

Greatest Annual Precipitation: 473 inches (1,200 cm) on the western part of South Island

Lowest Annual Precipitation: 11 inches (28 cm) on the eastern part of South Island

Hottest Recent Temperature: 94°F (34.1°C) at Timaru Airport on December 15, 1997

Lowest Recent Temperature: 16°F (-8.8°C) at Lauder on July 16, 1997

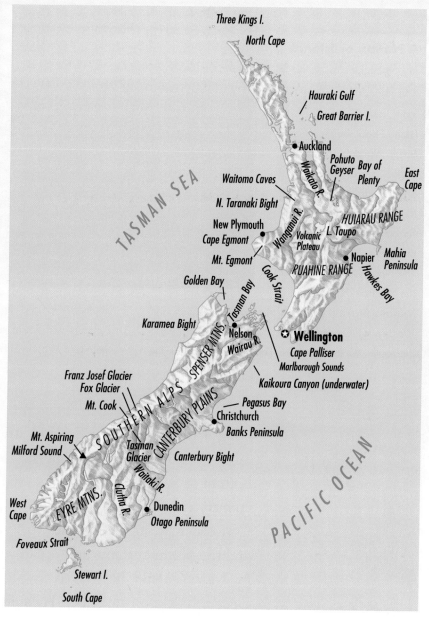

Greatest Distance North to South: 1,000 miles (1,610 km)

Greatest Distance East to West: 250 miles (402 km)

Most Populous City: Auckland: 1,050,000

A Nation of Islands

New Zealand is made up of 144 islands, including two main islands called North Island and South Island. South Island is the twelfth-largest island in the world and North Island is the fourteenth. These islands are surrounded by great expanses of ocean in all directions. The North Island consists of the Northern Peninsulas and Waikato Basin in the north; the Volcanic Region and Western Hill Country in the center of the island; and to the south, the Eastern Hills. The South Island has the Southern Alps and High Country in the west; the Otago Plateaus and Basins and the Canterbury Plains lie to the east.

The Lay of the Land

Long and narrow, New Zealand stretches nearly a thousand miles (1,610 kilometers) from the top at Cape Reinga to the bottom of Stewart Island. It is so narrow that no place in the country is farther than 75 miles (120 km) from the ocean. Consequently, its 3,200 miles (5,150 km) of ocean coastline and the ocean currents and ocean winds dominate Kiwi life.

New Zealand lies relatively alone in the South Pacific Ocean. Its closest neighbor, both emotionally and physically, is Australia, 1,000 miles (1,610 km) away. New Zealand is the other Down Under country. To the north lies the South Pacific island nations of New Caledonia, Fiji, and Tonga, who share a common Polynesian heritage with New Zealand. To the east, South America lies a far 5,000 miles (8,000 km) away and the United States is 6,500 miles (10,465 km) to the northeast. Although on a globe New Zealand looks so far south that it could float into Antarctica, it's really 2,000 miles (3,200 km) north of it. New Zealand runs from about the 34th parallel in the warmer north, to the 47th parallel in the colder south, roughly the same as Seattle to Los Angeles, or Quebec to Atlanta in the Northern Hemisphere.

New Zealand is a water-rich country, blessed with plentiful rain and mountain snows that feed its many rivers and lakes. Several mountain rivers, especially on the South Island, provide hydropower, irrigation water, and the perfect recipe for white-water rafting. Many North Island lakes are volcanic crater lakes while most lakes on the mountainous South Island are basin lakes.

Rafting a North Island river

Three-fourths of all New Zealanders live on North Island. It has the capital at Wellington, the business center at Auckland, warm beaches, and very fertile soil for farming and pastureland. That soil was born in New Zealand's volcanic history. Subtropical Northland was the first area to be settled both by the Maori and later by Europeans.

The First Sunrise

Because it lies just west of the international date line, New Zealand gets the jump on every other inhabited country. New Zealanders are the first to see each new day dawn. This location gives New Zealand prime importance for global events, such as celebrating the first dawn of the new millennium or tracking world trends. Financial analysts around the world eagerly watch the opening of New Zealand's stock exchange on days after the rest of the world has had extremely high or low trading.

The best part of being first is experiencing that new dawn. If you stand on top of Mount Hakepa in the Chatham Islands, 500 miles (800 km) east of South Island, you may be the first person in the world to see the brilliant scarlet line divide the black ocean from the black sky on a new day.

Further south, both dormant and active volcanoes mark New Zealand's landscape. The city of Auckland is dotted with old volcanic cones. Nearby in the Bay of Plenty, fiery eruptions continue to build Whakaari (White) Island. Mount Ruapehu, in the center of the North Island, recently erupted in 1996 and 1997. Other dramatic North Island volcanoes are Tongariro, Ngauruhoe, and Mount Egmont (Taranaki). Lake Taupo, the country's largest lake, fills a blasted-out crater that was formed by one of the largest explosions in history. The deep Wellington Harbor is a worn-away underwater crater. At Rotorua, in the center of the North Island, thermal pools and geysers bubble to the surface. Long ago, Maori cooked in these pools. For special events or picnics, some still do today. Accompanying all this volcanic activity are nearly 400, mostly small, earthquakes a year.

Mount Ruapehu erupting in the 1990s

Volcanoes and Earthquakes

Although volcanoes and earthquakes have done little damage in recent years, that wasn't the case in the past. More than 100 years ago, near the center of North Island at the edge of Lake Rotomahana, was a series of beautiful rose silica stone terraces. Water warmed by geothermal sources flowed over the steps and into the lake. Vacationers enjoyed sitting and bathing in the warm waters. The rose terraces sparkling in the sun were so beautiful and so extensive they became known as the eighth wonder of the natural world. That is, until June 10, 1886. That night Mount Tarawera unexpectedly erupted, blowing itself apart and burying nearby villages. The terraces were destroyed so completely not even a glint of rose was left. More than 150 people died.

Forty-five years later in 1931, a very strong earthquake, 7.9 on the Richter scale, destroyed much of Napier and Hastings on North Island's east coast. It was the worst quake in New Zealand modern history and killed 255 people. Napier has been beautifully rebuilt in art deco style which was very popular at the time the town was destroyed.

Experts predict within the next thirty years there will be another major quake somewhere offshore, near New Zealand. Earthquake-resistant building codes have been passed and the public is encouraged to become prepared for future earthquakes.

The Pacific Ring of Fire

○ Volcanoes, Ring of Fire
— Tectonic Plates

South Island

The mountain peaks, glaciers, lakes, and fjords of South Island's Westland, especially Milford Sound, are considered some of the most dramatic scenery in the world. These peaks descend to rocky shorelines deeply cut with long narrow fjord fingers. The west slopes of the Alps capture much of the moisture riding the westerlies across the Tasman Sea. The upper slopes are covered with thick snow and glaciers, the lower slopes with thick temperate rain forests.

Dramatic peaks tower over Milford Sound.

Skiers on Tasman Glacier in Mount Cook National Park

The Southern Alps are so rugged they have become a prime training ground for mountaineers practicing to climb Mount Everest and other Himalayan challenges. This glacier-capped range includes 223 mountain peaks higher than 7,500 feet (2,300 meters), and 16 above 10,000 feet (3,050 m). The tallest, Mount Cook at 12,349 feet (3,764 km), is on most mountaineers' list of peaks to conquer. On the lower slopes of the Alps in Fjordland National Park two of New Zealand's most famous tramping or hiking trails wind through the rain forest: the Milford and Routeburn tracks. The first European people to visit this area were seal hunters. One very homesick Welshman named the area Milford after his home in Wales.

Looking at New Zealand's Cities

Auckland, New Zealand's largest city, is located on an isthmus between Waitemata Harbor and Manukau Harbor on North Island. It is home to one of the world's largest population of Polynesian people. Founded in 1840, Auckland served as New Zealand's capital from that year until 1865. Today, the city is New Zealand's main port and main center of manufacturing. Major products made in Auckland factories include processed food, textiles, clothing, shoes, and automobiles. The University of Auckland attracts many New Zealanders. Visitors to the city enjoy exhibits at the New Zealand Maritime Museum and the Auckland City Art Gallery, as well as the sights in Auckland Domain, a large park in the center of the city.

Christchurch is a port city on the east coast of South Island. The city was founded by Anglican missionaries in 1850, and resembles the cities of Great Britain. Many of its homes have flower gardens. Today, Christchurch is known as one of the most English towns outside of England. Its downtown still has buildings from the mid-1800s. Cathedral Square is in the middle of the city, with Christchurch Cathedral in the middle of the square. Christchurch is an important New Zealand manufacturing center. Leading products include transportation equipment, carpets, woolens, and processed meat.

Manukau and North Shore are suburbs of Auckland. Manukau lies to the southwest on Manukau Harbor. Visitors there can tour Otuataua Stonefields, an archaeological site, to learn about early Maori and European settlement. They can also see the 66-foot (20-m) tall Millennium Sculpture, which portrays the importance of the family.

North Shore, which is northeast of Auckland, became a city in 1989. Today, it is New Zealand's fastest-growing city. Publishing and computer businesses are leading industries in North Shore. It is also known as a large retail center. Thousands of tourists visit North Shore each year, attracted by its parks and beaches. The America's Cup yacht race in 2000 was staged from the North Shore's harbor.

The Alps block much of the moisture from reaching the eastern side of South Island, making it drier and milder. In the center of the island on the Otago Plateau, miners discovered gold in 1861. This began a rush that gave a big population boom to the South Island. Until then most people lived on North Island. Beyond the Otago Plateau, the land eases into the flat fertile Canterbury Plains. Here, just the right amount of rain falls to provide good grazing land for dairy cows, sheep, and deer.

National Parks

New Zealand has thirteen national parks, nineteen national forests, three maritime and two marine parks, several nature reserves, and two World Heritage Sites—Tongariro National Park and Te Wahipounamu. World Heritage Sites are areas set

Tongariro National Park

aside for their special geological or historical significance. New Zealand's first national park, Tongariro, includes three volcano peaks and the surrounding area south of Lake Taupo in the center of North Island. Maori chief Ngati Tuwharetoa presented the parkland to the people of New Zealand in 1887 trusting them to protect this sacred and beautiful area. Te Wahipounamu includes several of the national parks of the Southern Alps—Fjordland, Mount Cook, Mount Aspiring, and Westland National Park.

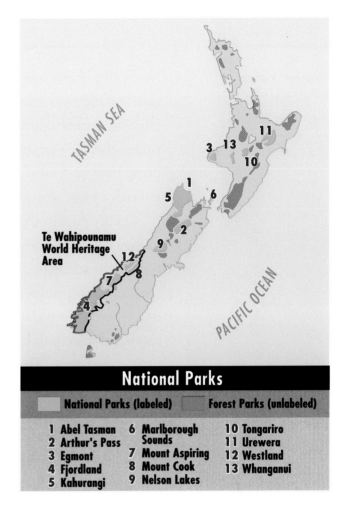

National Parks

National Parks (labeled)		Forest Parks (unlabeled)
1 Abel Tasman	6 Marlborough Sounds	10 Tongariro
2 Arthur's Pass	7 Mount Aspiring	11 Urewera
3 Egmont	8 Mount Cook	12 Westland
4 Fjordland	9 Nelson Lakes	13 Whanganui
5 Kahurangi		

It's a Fine Day

In New Zealand weather reports, the word fine is a term meaning sunny. With an average of 2,000 hours of sun a year, "fine" really does describe New Zealand's weather. The North Island is drier and warmer than the South Island. The very wettest part of the country is the west coast of South Island, where rainfall averages more than an inch a day. There is much less rain east of the mountains—only 11 inches (28 cm) compared with the 473 inches (1,200 cm) on the western slopes.

Year round, the weather is generally quite mild. Summers aren't too hot; winters not too cold. It rarely gets above 85°F (29°C), and snow rarely falls except in the mountains.

Normally, warm winds blow from the west. However, those gentle winds are sometimes overpowered by the "southerlies," chilling winds coming from the Antarctic south. At other times, the "nor'westerlies" blow in from the moist tropics and bring heat and rain. Sometimes they blow strong, even strong enough to become a cyclone.

On dry days in the Milford Sound area, three large waterfalls plunge down the fjord cliff walls. Sutherland Falls is the fifth-highest waterfall in the world. It flows downward 1,904 feet (580 m)—ten times taller than Niagara Falls. But on a stormy day, when the wind and rains pound the coast, as many as three thousand waterfalls pour down those cliffs. Many never make it to the sea below. The wind rushes in so violently, it blows the waterfalls sideways, and they become airborne mist.

Because New Zealand is in the southern hemisphere, the tilt of the earth is reversed from the northern hemisphere. When the northern hemisphere tilts away from the sun in winter, the southern hemisphere faces the sun more directly. This means that the seasons are reversed from the northern hemisphere. New Zealand experiences summer during December, January, and February. Winter comes in June, July, and August.

Clockwise and Counterclockwise Drains

Yes, water really does spin down drains clockwise south of the equator and counterclockwise north of it. This happens because the water, going down the drain, is pulled by gravity toward the earth's core. The earth always rotates toward the east. If you stood on the North Pole and looked down toward the earth's core, the earth would appear to rotate counterclockwise. If you're on the South Pole, the earth would appear to rotate clockwise. Stir a glass of water counterclockwise. Now hold the glass above your head, and keep stirring in the same direction. As you look up, the water will appear to be turning clockwise.

An Island of Birds

Millions of years ago all land masses of the Southern Hemisphere were part of one great continent, Gondwanaland. New Zealand was among the first blocks of land to break away and became isolated. At the time of the breakaway, mammals had not yet migrated to the Southern Hemisphere. When they did arrive finally, New Zealand was beyond their reach. With the exception of one species of bat, New Zealand remained a mammal-free island. Instead, it became a habitat for birds. Because of its isolation, New Zealand's birds are unique to New Zealand. Some plant and animal species have remained the same since New Zealand was part of Gondwanaland.

The takahe is a flight-less bird.

Leaving the Trees

Before people arrived in Aotearoa, the land was thickly forested with seed-producing trees and bushes and many kinds of insects, all abundant food for birds. With no mammals on the islands, there were few natural predators for the birds. They didn't have to fly to the treetops for safety. Over time some species left the trees for life on the food-rich ground. As the birds spent more and more time

on the ground, they were able to survive with smaller and weaker wings. Soon their wings were nothing more than stubby little appendages on fat round bodies. The birds lost the use of their wings entirely and could no longer fly. The kakapo, the world's largest parrot, and the kiwi are two kinds of birds that cannot fly, although they do have small wings.

People and Danger Arrive

When the Maori came to settle the islands, they brought dogs and rats for food. Later, European explorer Captain James Cook released wild pigs on the islands. These all ran free, feasting on birds' eggs and chicks. When they hunted ground birds, especially moas, sometimes the Maori burned areas of forest to force them out into the open. There, hunters easily surrounded and attacked the birds with clubs. However, burning the forests also destroyed both ground and tree nests. Soon many birds were endangered or extinct. Repeated fires in the same area also made it hard for the forest to recover, creating sweeping grasslands.

Birds of New Zealand

Fossils have shown that there were 106 different types of land and freshwater birds living in New Zealand before humans arrived. Nearly half have become extinct: thirty-five after the arrival of the Maori and another fourteen after the arrival of Europeans. Today some endangered birds are coming back under aggressive conservation programs. Offshore islands that have no predators have been set aside as wildlife reserves. The

Moa

The moa, similar to a giant ostrich, was once the world's largest bird. On average, it stood 12 feet (4 m) high and weighed 550 pounds (250 kg). Moas ate seeds, leaves, grasses, and fruits. The giant eagle was their only concern until man appeared. They were hunted to extinction by early Maori settlers. The Maori not only ate moa meat, they used the feathers for clothing, the bones for tools and carved decorations, and the empty egg shells as containers. Today, their skeletons (pictured), reconstructed moas, and moa artifacts are displayed in museums. Although the moas have been extinct for 500 years, during the last 150 years people have occasionally claimed to have seen a moa

in remote areas. Maybe it is a trick of the light, or an albatross standing on a large rock, or wishful thinking. Or perhaps there really are a few moas left in the rugged deep forests.

flightless takahe was thought to be extinct until 1948 when a few breeding pairs were found high in the South Alps, higher than most predators usually go. From the original birds found more than fifty years ago, there are nearly 200 now.

New Zealand has many endangered birds, however, other species are doing well. The tui, bellbird, and fantail are some of New Zealand's successful songbirds.

Although most of New Zealand's native birds are truly known only to the locals, two special birds have gained worldwide fame: the national bird, the kiwi, and the destructive mountain parrot, the kea. The kiwi is a round fuzzy brown nocturnal bird the size of a chicken. Its long thin bill probes the ground for insects during its night of hunting. To help find insects, its nose is at the end of its beak. Its brown feathers look almost like fluffy hair. Long ago the Maori used kiwi

Beneath the kea's drab green wings are bright scarlet feathers.

feathers to make warm, waterproof capes. The female kiwis lay their eggs and guard the nest, but the males sit on the nest, hatch the eggs, and care for the chicks. The name kiwi comes from the sound of the male's cry. There are three types of kiwi: brown, little spotted, and great spotted. The kiwis are a threatened species, but are doing well on the uninhabited outer islands where there are no predators.

The world's only mountain parrot, the kea, appears rather drab, green, and ordinary at first. Then it spreads its wings. The underside of its wings flash bright scarlet. Keas have a reputation for being bright, aggressive, curious, hungry, and destructive with their strong sharp beaks. They live in the high mountain forests of the South Island, but often hang around tourist destinations and restaurants hoping to be fed. If they aren't, they are likely to become vengeful, often attacking cars or ripping apart lawn furniture.

Animals of New Zealand

Besides birds and the bat, the tuatara lizard and many kinds of insects were early inhabitants of the islands. Fossils show that the tuatara has lived in New Zealand for millions of years. Of

A tuatara lizard

the estimated 20,000 kinds of insects in New Zealand, 90 per-cent are unique to the country. The weta, a cricket-like insect, grows to the size of a large mouse and is the world's largest insect. New Zealand is one of the few countries that has no snakes, and other than one rare spider, very few dangerous animals of any kind.

The weta is the largest insect in the world.

When European settlers came they brought plants and
animals from home. Many of these introduced animals, birds,
and plants have disrupted the natural balance of the islands,
often making it difficult or impossible for indigenous plants
and animals to survive. Rabbits, deer, possums, weasels, and
hedgehogs are among the introduced animals that have
thrived in New Zealand's mild climate. A shipment of rain-
bow-trout eggs, brought in from California in 1883, has
multiplied so much that rainbow trout now thrive in nearly all
lakes and rivers. But the native graying trout has disappeared.

Of all its animals, New Zealand may be most famous for its
sheep. From a distance, the 45 million sheep make hillside
pastures appear covered with patches of snow.

A country of contrast, New Zealand's green fields appear white with sheep and its deep caves on the North Island glow bright with worms. Glowworms cling to the ceilings of moist dark caves where their luminescent bodies shine, attracting insects. The worms release sticky threads that hang below them in the dark. Unsuspecting insects fly right into the threads, where they get caught and eaten. The glowworms are the larval stage of the fungus gnat.

Deep inside caves, glow-worms release sticky threads to capture insects.

Where Warm and Cold Waters Meet

Off the New Zealand shore the cold Antarctic currents meet the warm tropical currents. The meeting and mixing of these waters provides New Zealand with a rich variety of sealife. Several types of penguins burrow on the islands and feed at sea including the tiny blue penguin (also called fairy penguin), the fjordland crested penguin, and the rare yellow-eyed penguin. Giant albatross fly over the bays and far out to sea.

The waters off Kaikoura are the only place in the world where whales live in the same area year-round. Sperm whales, humpback whales, orca (killer) whales, and pilot whales are a few of the thirty-five kinds of whales that return offshore each year to breed. New Zealand and Australia are trying to establish a South Pacific sanctuary to protect the whale breeding grounds from nations hunting whales in the name of scientific research. They have had little success to date. Dolphins and seals are other common marine mammals that

Yellow-eyed penguins

inhabit New Zealand waters. Tuna, marlin, and shark come to New Zealand on the warm northern currents to feed on schools of smaller fish such as snapper, trevally, and kawhwai. Grouper, bass, salmon, sole, and mackerel all provide fishing jobs, food, and sport for Kiwis and visitors.

These fish are part of New Zealand's abundant sea life.

In the Ancient Forest

In the deep forest, a new fern frond coils just above the soil. When the rain stops and the sun slants through the tree

The Unseen Squid

New Zealand is even famous for animal life no one has ever seen alive—the giant squid. Although no one has seen one of these enormous creatures alive, their corpses have been found around the world drowned in fishing nets, washed up on beaches, and even in the stomachs of sperm whales. Scientists believe they have the best chance of seeing a living giant sea squid in the deep Kaikoura Canyon, off the east coast of South Island a half mile (1 km) underwater. These elusive squid can grow 60 feet long (18.3 m) and weigh a ton (907 kg). They have the largest eyes in the animal kingdom, 10 inches across (25.4 cm), about the size of a volleyball. Although timid, they have inspired monster tales such as *20,000 Leagues Under the Sea*.

Uncoiling fronds of tree ferns

branches, the coiled, brown, fuzzy frond will unfurl to the sky, becoming velvety green and long. The coiled brown frond is an important Maori symbol for renewal and growth. With much of the old forest cut and erosion a problem, renewal and growth are hopeful watchwords for New Zealand's forests.

Most of New Zealand's forests are thick and lush temperate rain forests. Large evergreen trees such as kauri and rimu, and lacy deciduous trees such as beech, overshadow and protect the undergrowth of shorter trees, bushes, ferns, and mosses. Vines connect everything. The forest floor is shady and protected.

Originally, 80 percent of Aotearoa was covered with forest. Of that, 84 percent of all the plants and 75 percent of the 2,000 kinds of flowering plants were not found anywhere else in the world. Most of the old forest was cut down for pasture and farm land or lumber long ago. Less than 25 percent of the original forest remains, covering only 15 percent of the land, mostly the mountain slopes of South Island and the distant reaches of Northland. The Northland forest has some of the oldest types of plants in the world. Scientists have found fossils that date from Gondwanaland that are similar to trees living now. Today the old forests are protected, but they are very difficult to expand. Vegetation imported by the early settlers chokes out the slower-growing native plants.

Unique Trees

The magnificent kauri tree (pictured) lives for 2,000 years; it is second only to California's sequoia redwoods in age. At 100 feet (30 m) it was a bonanza for early Maori looking for logs to carve for giant dugout canoes, called *wakas*. Later, loggers delighted in finding the large straight trees and quickly cut them for ship masts. Today, most of the Kauris are gone. Those that remain, mostly in Northland, are protected. Now only rarely is a tree cut, and only for some very special purpose, such as a Maori ceremonial canoe for the new museum.

The lovely 65-foot (20-m) high pohutukawa tree blooms brilliant red in December, giving it the nickname the Christmas Tree. It grows on lowlands, close to the sea, mostly on North Island.

A type of red pine, the rimu grows more than 160 feet (50 m) tall, creating a canopy over the lower forest. Once very common in lowland forests, wild rimu has been heavily harvested and is now rare. However, today rimu is sometimes planted on tree farms for lumber.

In this rain-rich land, there are over eighty-five types of ferns including fern trees. These tall ferns look almost like palm trees with fern fronds bunched at the top of a long trunk. The largest is the 65-foot (20-m) high mamaku, the black fern tree. Its fronds grow 20 feet (7 m) long. The ponga, the silver fern tree, grows 30 feet (10 m) tall. Its fronds grow 12 feet long (4 m) and are silver underneath and muted green on top. The outstretched silvery ponga frond has become a symbol of Kiwi spirit, sports, and their clean and green philosophy.

From Wilderness to Commonwealth

I N ANCIENT TIMES, LONG BEFORE THE HISTORY OF HUMANS, earthquakes and volcanoes shook Gondwanaland, the large continent near the bottom of the world. Eventually it broke apart to form all the Southern Hemisphere's landmasses. Part of one of the first pieces to crack away from Gondwanaland was a little split of land that would become present day New Zealand. For millions of years New Zealand lay apart in the ocean. Just over a thousand years ago, the Polynesians sailed far enough south to find the place they called Aotearoa, Land of the Long White Cloud.

Opposite: **The legendary departure of the Maori ancestors from Hawaiki**

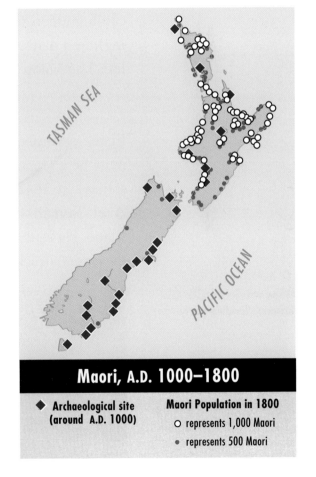

Settling Aotearoa

Maori legend tells that hundreds of years later, perhaps around A.D. 1300, their Polynesian ancestors set sail to find a new home. They came from islands probably in Micronesia called Hawaiki. They knew of Aotearoa, from oral-history stories about the great Polynesian navigator Kupe's journey and discovery. The Maori settled on North Island and found the rich and abundant land undisturbed since the days of Gondwanaland.

Maori, A.D. 1000–1800

◆ **Archaeological site (around A.D. 1000)**

Maori Population in 1800
- ○ represents 1,000 Maori
- • represents 500 Maori

The Maori settled in separate tribes. Each tribe had its own strong society. There was no leader for all Maori. Instead the tribes had either friendly or hostile relations with their neighboring tribes. When encountering members of a different tribe, they did a challenge dance called a *haka*, which could turn into a welcome dance for members of a friendly tribe. They waged war with enemy tribes, and even took slaves.

The Maori lived as hunters and gatherers and raised crops such as taro root and kumara sweet potatoes. Art, especially carving greenstone and wood, weaving, skin design (tattooing), and dance were, and still are, important parts of Maori life. The Maori valued strength, bravery, and hunting skills.

Europeans Find Aotearoa

In the seventeenth century many Europeans believed there must be a great continent somewhere in the southern hemisphere. In 1642, while searching for it, the Dutch explorer Abel Tasman sailed to the west coast of Aotearoa's South Island. He sent a scouting party to explore, but before landing they were attacked by Maori in a war canoe. Four of Tasman's

Maori warriors attack Abel Tasman's landing party.

men were killed and eaten. Captain Tasman quickly sailed up the west coast and did not land again. Because he sailed only along the west coast he believed he had found the Pacific coast of South America. The next year other Dutch explorers in the South Pacific realized Aotearoa was not South America. The Dutch named the land discovered by Tasman *Nieuw Zeeland* after the Zeeland province in the Netherlands.

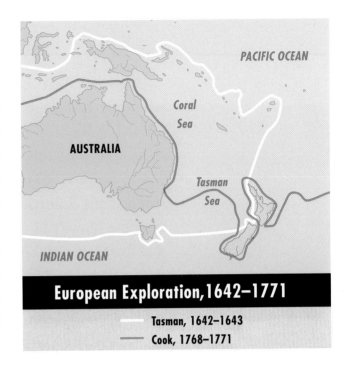

European Exploration,1642–1771

— Tasman, 1642–1643
— Cook, 1768–1771

Captain James Cook (1728-1779)

Captain James Cook was one of England's foremost and fearless explorers. He made three voyages exploring and mapping the Pacific from the Bering Sea to Antarctica. On two voyages he circled the world. During the third, he was killed by natives in Hawaii.

As a teenager he learned about sailing working on coal-delivery ships. He wrote that he wanted "not only to go farther than anyone had done before, but as far as possible for man to go." He joined the British navy where he learned surveying and map-making along the St. Lawrence River and the Canadian coast. His reports were well detailed, and soon he became a captain. He visited New Zealand in 1769, on his first world voyage. He returned on both his other journeys. His name marks geological features around the world including Cook Strait, the waterway that separates North Island and South Island, and Mount Cook.

Europeans left Aotearoa and the Maori alone until 1769 when the British seaman and explorer Captain James Cook arrived in his ship the *Endeavour*. Cook drew maps so good they were used for decades. When he landed he met with Maori warriors. Cook was able to communicate with them through his Tahitian interpreter and was greatly impressed with the bravery of the Maori. During several meetings Cook and the Maori established a good relationship and began trading for supplies. After noting their promise as a colony, Cook claimed the islands for Great Britain. About the same time, French explorers were sailing around the islands and claiming the land for France.

The Sealers and Whalers Bring Trouble

The first Europeans to regularly visit the islands of Aotearoa were sailors from European ships hunting seals for their oil and skin. The Maori called these pale-skinned people *pakeha*, meaning colorless.

By the end of the 1700s, all the seals in the area were killed. Then the Europeans hunted whales until they also were gone. The sealers, whalers, and sailors came ashore to trade with the Maori for food, wood, and water and to hire the strong Maori men to work on their ships. At first they traded trinkets, but later they offered alcohol, metal tools, and guns for supplies and souvenir Maori shrunken heads and weapons. These men enjoyed visiting this country which had no government and no laws. They came from around the world: France, Spain, the United States, and the British Isles.

Some were pirates and some escaped Australian convicts. Usually trade went smoothly. If the Maori felt, however, that they were treated unfairly, violent conflicts could ensue.

As with most native people around the world, early contact with Europeans turned disastrous for the Maori. The European sailors loved the Maori preserved heads of their enemies. They would trade almost anything for them. The Maori wanted these goods and used their new guns to kill members of enemy tribes to get a supply of heads. This and diseases brought by the European sailors quickly led to a crash of Maori population. Within fifty years of European presence, the Maori population fell by half.

The trade in human heads was disastrous for the Maori.

Missionaries Arrive in Aotearoa

Other than the few sailors and traders that had settled on the islands, the first European settlers were missionaries. The Reverend Samuel Marsden led the first group of twenty-one families to Aotearoa in 1814. They settled near Russell in the subtropical area of the Bay of Islands on North Island. Marsden had intended to teach the Maori British farming methods. He brought horses which frightened the Maori, grains which puzzled them with their lack of edible roots, and plows which disturbed them, for they believed plow cuts hurt the earth.

Reverend Samuel Marsden (1765–1838)

The Reverend Samuel Marsden was a judge in Sydney where he was known as "the flogging parson," because that was his favorite punishment to order. In Sydney he met Maori warriors who were working on whaling ships. He was impressed with their loyalty and strength and stories of Aotearoa. In 1814 he led a group of missionaries to Aotearoa to convert the Maori and teach them English farming methods. This was the first European settlement. Marsden became the first pakeha to officially buy Maori land. In 1815 he bought 200 acres at the Bay of Islands for twelve iron axes.

Historical portrait of a Maori chief

When the missionaries saw the beautiful country, many quickly forgot their Christian intent and became more interested in taking Maori land. Some missionaries began dealing in guns and alcohol and were disrespectful of Maori traditions and beliefs. Soon they were trying to take Maori land, at very unfair prices, if they paid at all.

The Maori didn't believe that land could be owned by an individual. Each tribe cooperatively held territory. They didn't understand what a land sale meant in British law, because there was no equivalent in Maori tradition. When sales did take place, the Maori thought they were allowing use, or leasing the land, but that the land remained tribal territory. Sometimes one tribe would raid another tribe and chase them from their own land. Then they would sell the land to pakehas. When the other tribe returned, they often found missionaries or settlers claiming their tribal land. The Maori weren't allowed to live on it or even cross it.

Although lawlessness continued to be the rule on Aotearoa, some missionaries did remain true to their Christian beliefs. They feared for the Maori people and continually petitioned England to establish laws and take control. Unexpectedly, they had allies in the whalers and farmers. There was a heavy import tax to ship whale oil and wool to England since Aotearoa was considered a foreign country. In 1817 England decided to add New Zealand to the territory governed by New South Wales in Australia, 1,500 miles (2,500 km) away. Eventually a British representative from Australia was stationed in Russell. However, he was so powerless and ineffective the Maori called him the "man of war without guns."

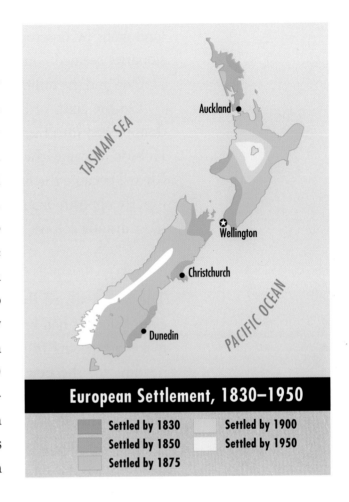

European Settlement, 1830–1950

Settled by 1830 Settled by 1900
Settled by 1850 Settled by 1950
Settled by 1875

Aotearoa Turns Into New Zealand

As more settlers emigrated from England, missionaries pleaded for help in establishing order from the British government. Finally, in 1839 the English sent Captain William Hobson of the navy to take control of the islands. First, he needed to make a treaty with the Maori. By this time Maori society was suffering severely from the lawlessness, European diseases, and land grabs by unscrupulous Europeans. Only some of the missionaries seemed concerned with their welfare. To the Maori, Hobson and the military were trusted friends of the missionaries.

On the sixth of February the treaty was signed. Aotearoa disappeared into history and New Zealand emerged. Captain Hobson became the first governor of the new colony and Russell became the first capital. New Zealand, which is almost exactly opposite from Great Britain on the globe, became its most distant colony.

The Land Wars

The Maori signed the treaty to protect their land. However, even before it had been written, British companies hoping to make big profits from Maori land had boats full of settlers heading for the new colony. Funds to run the New Zealand government were scarce and there was little money to make proper payments to the Maori for their land. However, many new settlers had plenty of money to buy land. The government started raising money by buying Maori land far below its value and reselling it at high prices to settlers.

Although many Maori tried to limit how much land could be sold, the government forced them to sign over more and more land. The government often paid the Maori less than 5 percent of what they resold the land for. Other times, the government supported new settlers who claimed to have bought land from someone who bought it from the Maori before the treaty was signed. Soon, the Maori felt so angry and cheated they attacked and killed British troops at Waitara.

The Treaty of Waitangi and *Te Tiriti o Waitangi*

No document is more important to New Zealand than the Treaty of Waitangi. This agreement between the British Crown and the Maori chiefs is the founding document of New Zealand. It guides the country today.

In February 1840, Captain Hobson gathered with forty-five tribal chiefs at Waitangi on the Bay of Islands. They came to create a treaty that would give Great Britain the right to officially be in New Zealand and protect Maori interests. After days of discussion they agreed that Great Britain would form the government of New Zealand, and the ruler of Great Britain, then Queen Victoria, would be the official leader. The Maori would receive full rights given to all British citizens. To protect Maori land rights, it could be sold only to the government at fair prices. The government then would resell the land to settlers for a small profit. This would ensure the Maori wouldn't be swindled.

On February 6, the treaty was signed. With a twenty-one-gun salute, Aotearoa became New Zealand. The treaty was then taken throughout the country and eventually signed by over 500 tribal chiefs. But not all the chiefs signed, and it was never officially approved by Great Britain.

Almost immediately the simple agreement became very complicated. There were two copies of the treaty—one in Maori and one in English. However, the translations were not the same. In the English version, the Maori gave full control of their country to Great Britain. The Maori version gave the British government a governorship rather than full control. The different interpretations are the difference between surrender and an alliance. This difference led to many arguments that continue today. Some land has been returned to the Maori. They have been more properly paid for other land. Other disputes will be in the courts for many years to come.

This sparked battles between tribes and the military around the islands. In the first ten years after the treaty, the Maori lost 50 percent of their land.

The Maori had always acted as individual tribes and had no single leader. This made negotiating with the new government more difficult, especially since the tribes were often enemies themselves. In 1856 William Thompson, a respected Maori chief, proposed to the governor that the Maori form their own government. The governor liked having one less worry. In 1858 Te Wherowhero was chosen as king. A council of advisers was appointed to help him unite the tribes. This began the King Movement. Land was set aside where no pakeha were allowed. Unity strengthened the tribes. Although they still disagreed about some things, the tribes no longer considered other tribes enemies.

Gold prospectors

Twenty years after the signing of the Treaty of Waitangi, gold was discovered in the gravel river beds of the Otago region of South Island. Miners from around the world rushed to find their fortunes. The gold strike ended quickly, leaving most people as poor as when they arrived. Although most miners moved onto other strikes in other places, some stayed to farm, creating even more demand for land. The lush meadows of the Canterbury Plains proved to be wonderful for sheep and cattle grazing. The new settlers began clearing the forest and soon New Zealand logs, wool, and wheat were being shipped around the British Empire.

The Maori continued to be treated unfairly in many ways after the treaty was signed. Although the treaty gave the Maori citizenship and voting rights, British law allowed only male landowners to vote. Because the tribe owned the land, Maori men weren't allowed to vote and had no representation in government. When Maori wanted bank loans for farm equipment or to buy livestock, the banks wouldn't lend them money

A battle in the Land Wars

because they had no individual titles to their land or farm. The Maori were often met with discrimination. Finally, in 1867 Maori men were allowed to vote and four seats in Parliament were set aside to represent Maori.

In the 1860s and 1870s, the pressure to sell and the unfairness of land deals led to more violent conflicts between the Maori, the government, and the settlers. Some battles were fierce surprise attacks in

Hone Heke (?–1850)

Chief Hone Heke, a leader of the Ngapuhi tribe, was the first Maori to sign the Treaty of Waitangi. However, when he saw all flags but the British flag taken down, he knew it would not be good for the Maori. He worked to help the Maori hold onto their land and was a leading warrior in the early land wars. He chopped down the British flagpole at Russell (Kororareka) as the first act of Maori defiance. Heke managed to chop down the flagpole four times although the British clad it in iron and heavily guarded it. He and his warriors burned Russell (Kororareka) forcing the British residents to flee to boats in the harbor. After that the capital was moved to Auckland. Governor George Grey offered a one hundred British pound reward (a great deal of money then) for Chief Hone Heke's head. The chief responded by offering one hundred pounds for the governor's head. A monument to Heke has been erected at Kaikohe where he died in 1850 with his head intact.

which soldiers, settlers, and Maori all died. Sometimes the Maori held nonviolent protests such as burning flagpoles. Most of the fighting was in central North Island. Although not all tribes participated, all Maori shared concerns about land sales. After several years of battling and burned settlements, the wars tapered off in the early 1870s and officially ended in 1881. This time is called the Land Wars or the New Zealand Wars.

Building a Nation

By the end of the 1870s, a half million people lived in New Zealand. Most were farmers. With the abundance of lush grassy pastures, most people raised sheep for wool. Roads and railroads were being built across the land to help take the wool to seaports. In 1882, a new invention changed the farm business in New Zealand and in all the world. Refrigerated ships allowed frozen meat to be shipped to England. Suddenly sheep weren't just for wool. The meat could also be sold to England.

The New Zealand economy boomed. More people immigrated to start dairy and sheep farms, and more New Zealand goods were shipped around the world.

After the Land Wars, peace and prosperity prevailed. In 1865 Great Britain gave New Zealand the right to establish its own parliamentary government, with the Queen of England as head. This new independence allowed New Zealand to turn its attention to making the country a progressive nation on many fronts. Laws were passed for worker protection, minimum wage, child health care, and government loans to buy farms.

In 1893 New Zealand became the first country in the world to allow women to vote. In 1898 it introduced old age pensions. New Zealand no longer needed financial or military support from Great Britain, but historical and cultural ties held them together. In 1907 the British crown granted New Zealand's request for "dominion status"—the right to be a self-governed country within the British Empire, rather than a colony.

The Maori didn't make the same movement forward. By the end of the century the Maori population fell to 42,000, less than a quarter of its pre-European population of 200,000–300,000. The use of Maori language and traditions were discouraged by the government and the culture seemed to be dying.

Into the Twentieth Century

The outbreak of World War I pulled New Zealand onto the world arena in a big way. More than 100,000 Kiwi soldiers went to fight on foreign shores, while the rest of the country

Scientist Ernest Rutherford

Aviator Jean Batten

produced dairy, meat, produce, and wool to support the troops. During the war, New Zealand's prosperity soared. However, by the end of the war most Kiwis believed the price of war prosperity was too high. New Zealand soldiers suffered more casualties per capita than any other nation. One-third of all New Zealand men between ages 20 and 40 were injured or killed. April 25, 1915, the beginning of a battle in Turkey where many Kiwis died, has become ANZAC (Australia-New Zealand Army Corps) Day, a national day of remembrance.

After World War I, the economic depression creeping around the world settled down hard on New Zealand. Prices for farm products dropped by 40 percent on the world market. As an agricultural, exporting country, New Zealand lost much of its income. People lost their jobs and homes. Life became uncertain and difficult. Riots demanding help broke out on the streets of Auckland. By 1934 prices began to rise, and in 1935 Kiwis elected a new government. The government set a forty-hour workweek and guaranteed good farm prices, excellent health care for everyone, and housing programs to help make sure people would have less suffering and worry in the future.

During the first part of the twentieth century individual Kiwis made their own marks on world history: Scientist Ernest Rutherford split the atom and won the Nobel Prize, and Jean Batten broke many aviation records with her flying. In 1953 Sir Edmund Hillary summitted Mount Everest. Hillary's accomplishment brought worldwide attention to the mountainous country where he trained and lived.

U.S. and New Zealand troops during World War II

World War II and the Years After

As war swept into the South Pacific, New Zealand again provided soldiers and support. Nearly 10 percent of the population, including Maori troops, fought overseas. After the war, with Europe's farms in ruins, New Zealand's agriculture was in great demand around the world. For the next two decades, the economy boomed as agricultural production increased and new industries developed.

As most of New Zealand moved enthusiastically into the post-war years, discontentment grew among the Maori. Many young Maori migrated from traditional villages into cities for work. There they became distanced even further from their culture. After World War II cultural pride and equal rights movements spread in many western countries, such as the civil rights and Native American rights movements in the United States. In the 1970s young Maori who lived in the cities began a movement to reclaim their heritage. This had support from Maori, pakeha, and the government. Maori language and traditions became a valued part of New Zealand's character and heritage, valued not only by Maori, but by all New Zealanders.

During the 1970s, New Zealand's zooming economy hit two severe speed bumps. New Zealand imports most of its natural minerals and petroleum. The 1970s fuel crisis hit New Zealand hard. Gasoline supplies became unreliable and expensive. At the same time Great Britain, New Zealand's main trading partner, joined the European Community's Common Market. This changed British taxation policies and limited how much trade-goods could be imported from New Zealand. Trade between New Zealand and Great Britain became much more expensive and trade between Britain and Europe became much cheaper. Fortunately, a new source of income began to grow. International travel became affordable for many more people and tourists began traveling to New Zealand.

In spite of budget worries, New Zealand continued to support social reforms and human rights. The government supported Maori cultural awareness, banned homosexual discrimination and capital punishment, and supported environmental protection. It took until the 1990s before the economy began a strong recovery.

Environmental issues have become very important to New Zealanders. In the early days of European settlement forested hills were clear-cut for sheep farms and grain crops. This led to severe erosion and flooding problems. Rain washed away valuable topsoil, clogging streams and rivers. A Department of

Conservation was established in the 1970s along with programs for reforestation and protective planting. The remaining natural forest was protected where possible. Protection programs for endangered birds were started. Hydroelectric power was developed with much more care and scrutiny. And after the *Rainbow Warrior* protest ship exploded, all nuclear sources of power and nuclear weapons were banned from New Zealand and its waters.

The *Rainbow Warrior*

After World War II, France began testing nuclear bombs on Mururoa, a South Pacific island under its protection. This worried New Zealanders because of possible accidents and the danger of nuclear radiation blowing their way. In spite of strong protests, France continued the tests. In 1985, Greenpeace, the international environmental organization, had a ship, the *Rainbow Warrior* docked in the Auckland harbor. It was to lead a flotilla of protest ships to Mururoa. The night before the journey started, the *Rainbow Warrior* exploded and sank in the harbor. One person died. Two French spies were later convicted of the crime. After much negotiation and worldwide condemnation, France apologized and paid restitution. New Zealand turned the spies over to France, where they were to finish their imprisonment. However, they were released and given special honors. In 1995 France briefly resumed nuclear testing on Mururoa.

The incident reinforced New Zealand's idea that it wanted nothing to do with nuclear power or weapons. In 1985, it voted to make itself a nuclear-free zone and banned all ships that carried nuclear weapons or were nuclear powered from its waters. These ships included those of its allies, Australia and the United States. New Zealanders take a great deal of pride in their stand against world powers for what they believe is right.

New Zealand Now and in the Future

New Zealanders have very valued and strong ties to Great Britain and to the British Crown. They were delighted when Queen Elizabeth agreed to visit their country in 1995 and open the magnificent Te Papa national museum. However, the ties are weakening. Kiwis have created their own national personality, values, and lifestyle quite different from those of Mother England. In a move away from Great Britain, they changed their currency from the NZ pound to the NZ dollar in 1967.

Australia recently voted whether to sever ties with the British Commonwealth and become a Republic. The bill didn't pass because it didn't allow people to directly elect their prime minister. When this is added, it is expected that the bill will pass. New Zealanders predict they will follow in Australia's footsteps and become a republic rather than remain a member of the British Commonwealth. More and more New Zealanders believe their future lies as an independent country on the world arena and in alliances with their Australian and Asian Pacific neighbors.

New Zealand has become an important part of the peace-keeping forces of the United Nations and its soldiers serve in places like Bosnia, the Middle East, Asia, and Africa. It has taken leadership peacekeeping roles especially in the South Pacific in places such as Timor and Fiji. The country has a strong interest in seeing that its area of the world remains peaceful and economically secure.

In the meantime there is a new energy and optimism developing in New Zealand. It is fueled by Kiwi pride;

by hopeful immigrants coming from North America, Australia, and Southeast Asia; by new agriculture, especially new varieties of apples, gourmet cheeses, and wine; by growing worldwide tourism; and by new technology industries.

New Zealand soldiers honor one of their own killed during a peace keeping mission.

Two Queens and a Parliament

ALTHOUGH NEW ZEALAND IS A CONSTITUTIONAL monarchy, it has two queens and no constitution. In 1840, the Treaty of Waitangi between the Maori and Great Britain made the British monarch, then Queen Victoria, the official head of government. She appointed a governor-general to oversee the everyday running of the country. Later the individual Maori tribes banded together and elected their own royal leaders and advisers. Today, New Zealand is a true bi-cultural nation and has two official languages, English and Maori. New Zealand is a member of the British Commonwealth, a cooperative organization of former British colonies and nations once under British rule.

Opposite: **Waitangi Treaty House**

Government office buildings in Wellington

Organizing the Government

In 1852, Great Britain gave New Zealand a constitution and the right to govern itself. However, the queen's governor-general remained in place. Over the years, nearly all of the original constitution has been changed, leaving New Zealand without a constitution. Today, the governing documents of New Zealand are its Acts of Parliament. The Treaty of Waitangi is considered the founding document of New Zealand. February 6, the day it

Two Queens

Queen Elizabeth (above) and Queen Te Atairangikaahu (right) are the current monarchs of New Zealand. Although neither has political power, both are greatly respected by all New Zealanders, and both have considerable social and political influence. In 1966, Queen Te Atairangikaahu ended the line of exclusive Maori kings, when a gathering of chiefs chose her to become monarch.

was first signed, has become Waitangi Day, when New Zealanders celebrate the founding of their country.

New Zealanders have great faith and trust in their government. In 2000, New Zealand was rated the third least corrupt government in the world. It is considered one of the most progressive countries in the world, offering many benefits to its citizens. Also in 2000, New Zealand was rated the ninth-best country for supporting women's concerns. This reflects a long and continuing tradition. New Zealand was the first country

NATIONAL GOVERNMENT OF NEW ZEALAND

Executive
- PRIME MINISTER
- CABINET
- EXECUTIVE COUNCIL
- MINISTERS (DEPARTMENT HEADS)

Legislature
- MEMBERS OF PARLIAMENT

Honorary
- THE BRITISH MONARCH
- GOVERNOR-GENERAL

Judiciary
- PRIVY COUNCIL
- COURT OF APPEAL
- HIGH COURT
- DISTRICT COURT

to give women the vote. In 2001 the prime minister, leader of the opposition, governor-general, and the chief high court judge positions were all held by women.

New Zealand's government and many of its institutions are patterned after those in Great Britain. Legally, Queen Elizabeth remains the head of government. However, she and her appointed representative, the governor-general, have no power. Their role is ceremonial. The power lies with the prime minister and the elected members of Parliament.

The minimum voting age is 18 and registering to vote is mandatory. However, no one is actually required to vote. Voting is held on a Saturday and all registered voters who have been in the country at least a year may vote. Not to be denied their say, about 80 percent of all registered voters do go to the polls.

Parliament

When Great Britain originally gave New Zealand a constitution, New Zealand had two representative bodies—an honorary upper house consisting of people appointed by the queen or governor-general and a lower house of elected members. New Zealanders quickly eliminated the honorary members. Now, a single Parliament body functions as a house of representatives.

In 1993 New Zealand adopted a mixed member proportional (MMP) electoral system, similar to that in Germany. Parliament is made up of 120 members. Sixty seats represent regions. Fifty-five seats are voted on nationwide to represent political parties. Each person receives two votes—one for his or her regional

Parliament buildings. The Beehive is on the left.

representative and one for a representative of the political party he or she wants to control Parliament. Five seats are reserved for Maori representatives. Those registered as Maori may vote for either a nationwide Maori candidate or for the member of their region, in addition to a party candidate. Maori may also hold any other regional and party seats.

The party with the majority of members of Parliament gets to install their party leader as prime minister. If no party has a majority, they may form a partnership with another party to gain control of the prime minister position and cabinet. This gives smaller parties a powerful position in forming coalition governments and having their concerns heard. The prime minister must be an elected member of Parliament.

Winston Peters is a founder of the New Zealand First Party.

Political Parties

The two main parties are the Nationals (similar in philosophy to the United States Republican Party) and the Labour Party (similar to the Democratic Party). Both parties have common concerns and goals, but different approaches and styles. If a party gets 5 percent of the vote, they will receive a seat in Parliament. The Green Party and the New Zealand First Party are two of the more widely supported smaller factions. Several other minor parties grouped together to form the Alliance Party.

The Executive

New Zealand is led by a prime minster (PM), a position similar to a president. However, the prime minister is not directly elected by the people. The person holding the position of leadership within the party that gets the majority support in the past election becomes prime minister. People know before they vote who each party will install as PM if the party wins the majority of votes.

The prime minister chooses a cabinet of advisers who manage various departments of government. The departments—such as labor, finance, and education—are called portfolios. The cabinet members are called ministers of portfolios. Together with the prime minister, they are referred to as the government. When a new party wins control, it is referred to as a new government. The prime minister and all cabinet members are also members of Parliament.

Every three years New Zealanders hold national elections for Parliament and prime minister. If the people believe the government isn't doing a good job before the next election, a majority of Parliament can call for a vote of confidence. If the government fails to get the support of a majority of Parliament, new elections are held.

Prime Minister Helen Clark

From the time she was a young girl growing up in Hamilton, Helen Clark was passionate about being involved. While a political science student at Auckland University, she joined the Labour Party because of her concerns about the Vietnam War, apartheid in South Africa, women's issues, and nuclear testing in the South Pacific. After getting her Ph.D, she taught politics at the university. In 1981 she was elected to Parliament from Mount Albert in Auckland. Since then she has served in many positions in the party. She was elected prime minister on November 27, 1999. She is also currently the minister for arts, culture, and heritage. Her agenda includes broadening New Zealand's commodity-based economy to embrace a larger knowledge base, with more technology, science, and engineering.

Although she has a very demanding schedule, PM Clark fits in music, the opera, theater, and like most New Zealanders, as much outdoor activity as she can. In 1999 she climbed Mount Kilimanjaro. Her husband, Peter Davis, is a professor at the university in Christchurch. They have no children.

When PM Clark talks with young people she encourages them to make the most of their lives. To do this she advises: develop self-confidence; set goals and concentrate on getting there; understand it takes work, discipline, and organization to reach goals; develop a sense of humor and tolerance; support others and make sure you get support; make time for family, for friends, and for fun.

Without a constitution, New Zealand's laws are based on the English Bill of Rights. People are always presumed innocent until they are found guilty in a court of law. Decisions can be appealed to a higher court. All judges and prosecutors are appointed, not elected.

A police officer on duty

Minor disputes and crimes are heard in local courts called district courts. The High Court hears serious crimes and appeals from the district courts. Above the High Court is the Court of Appeal and finally the Privy Court, the nation's highest judicial body. The Privy Court only hears cases sent up by lower courts. The Waitangi Tribunal was established in 1975 to handle Maori land claims and issues relating to the Treaty of Waitangi.

The laws of New Zealand are enforced by 6,000 police who do not wear guns and a voluntary military force of 11,000 men and women. The death penalty was outlawed in the 1960s.

Ombudsmen

New Zealand has a government-appointed ombudsman who represents the people in disputes with the government. The ombudsman investigates complaints against

70 *New Zealand*

governmental departments and tries to help both parties reach a solution. This is a very respected and important position in New Zealand's government.

The Capital

In the early days, Russell (Kororareka) in Northland acted as capital. After signing the Treaty of Waitangi, Governor Hobson decided to move the capital to the protective harbor at Auckland. In 1865 to help unify the two islands,

Modern offices in Wellington

Wellington: Did You Know This?

Population: 329,000 (2001)

Year Founded: 1840

Altitude: Sea level

Average Daily Temperature: 68°F (20°C) in January 42°F (5.6°C) in July

Average Annual Rainfall: 50 inches (127 cm)

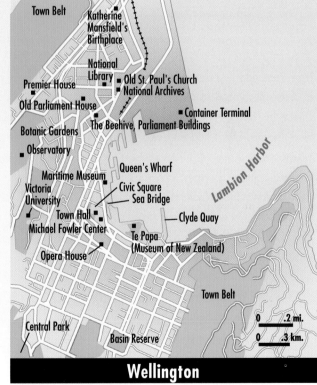

Town Belt
Katherine Mansfield's Birthplace
National Library
Old St. Paul's Church
National Archives
Premier House
Old Parliament House
Container Terminal
The Beehive, Parliament Buildings
Botanic Gardens
Observatory
Queen's Wharf
Maritime Museum
Victoria University
Civic Square
Sea Bridge
Town Hall
Clyde Quay
Michael Fowler Center
Te Papa (Museum of New Zealand)
Opera House
Lambton Harbor
Town Belt
0   .2 mi.
0   .3 km.
Central Park
Basin Reserve

Wellington

National Anthem: "God Defend New Zealand"

New Zealand has two national anthems. The first, "God Save the Queen," became official at the signing of the Treaty of Waitangi. In 1876 a contest was held to set music to Thomas Bracken's poem "God Defend New Zealand." The new song, with music by Otago school teacher John Joseph Woods, was performed in Dunedin that Christmas. It was a hit. In 1878 it was translated into Maori. With the queen's approval, the song was promoted from national hymn to co-national anthem in 1977. Today it is sung in both English and Maori.

English

God of Nations! at Thy feet,
In the bonds of love we meet,
Hear our voices we entreat,
God defend our free land
Guard Pacific's triple star
From the shafts of strife and war,
Make her praises heard afar,
God defend New Zealand.

Mäori

E Ihowä Atua,
O ngä iwi mätouä
Äta whakarongona;
Me aroha noa
Kia hua ko te pai;
Kia tau tö atawhai;
Manaakitia mai
Aotearoa.

New Zealand's Flag

New Zealand's flag developed from the need to have its ships recognized at sea. The first official flag was chosen in 1835 by a group of Maori chiefs. It resembled the missionary flag and was called Flag of the Independent Tribes of New Zealand. When New Zealand became a colony, England's flag, the Union Jack, became New Zealand's flag as well. In 1865 England ordered all its colonies to use a blue flag with their own seal on it. Because it had no seal, the governor ordered the letters NZ in red surrounded by a white border put on the flag. No one liked the design. In 1869 a new governor replaced the NZ with the four main stars of the Southern Cross, using the same colors.

Although it was a maritime flag, people also used it on land instead of England's Union Jack. To avoid the confusion of having two flags, New Zealand adopted its present design in 1902. The flag illustrates New Zealand's history and position in the world. In the upper left is a small Union Jack. On the body of the flag, the four stars of the Southern Cross constellation fly against a field of dark blue, just as the stars shine against New Zealand's southern night sky.

it moved again to its present location of Wellington.

The capitol complex consists of several buildings in downtown Wellington on a hill overlooking the harbor. By far the most famous and controversial structure is the parliamentary office building, the Beehive. It is loved or loathed by New Zealanders. All agree, however, that this tiered, circular building built in the 1970s, is innovative architecture. It is currently being remodeled.

Local Government

New Zealand is divided into twelve political regions, each with an elected council, and four unitary authorities, which also have a regional government. Each region is further divided into towns or districts. Each town and district also has its own local council, headed by an elected mayor.

In reality though, this is a country of just under 4 million people in about the same square miles as Colorado. Local issues easily become national issues. Most citizens know their member of Parliament and expect them to help smooth the governmental way in life. And whenever possible, the MPs do.

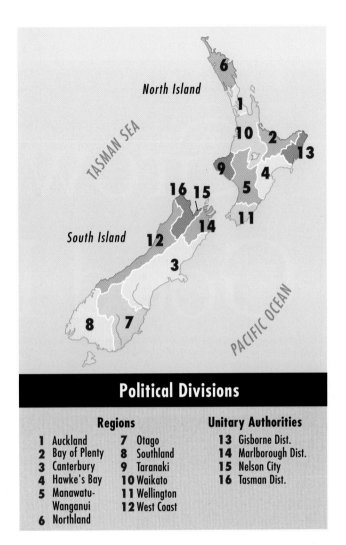

Political Divisions

Regions

1	Auckland	7	Otago
2	Bay of Plenty	8	Southland
3	Canterbury	9	Taranaki
4	Hawke's Bay	10	Waikato
5	Manawatu-Wanganui	11	Wellington
6	Northland	12	West Coast

Unitary Authorities

13	Gisborne Dist.
14	Marlborough Dist.
15	Nelson City
16	Tasman Dist.

Growing a Good Living

D RIVING PAST NEW ZEALAND'S PASTURES AND ORCHARDS, it's easy to see the economic backbone of the country. In all of New Zealand nothing is more valuable than the rich soil and the abundant rain and sun. Together they fuel the economy. New Zealand is expanding its economic base, especially in the knowledge and information industry, in manufacturing, and in tourism. But for now it remains primarily an agricultural economy.

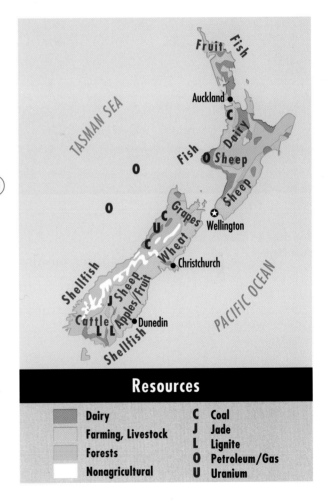

Resources

⬛	Dairy	**C**	Coal
⬜	Farming, Livestock	**J**	Jade
⬜	Forests	**L**	Lignite
⬜	Nonagricultural	**O**	Petroleum/Gas
		U	Uranium

What Grows and Where It Goes

New Zealand has 70,000 farms with more than 40 million acres (16.6 million hectares) of land under cultivation. Unlike other agricultural countries, about 65 percent of New Zealand farms are small, under 250 acres (104 ha). Three-fourths of these are owned by families, rather than businesses. Of the land under cultivation, half is pasture for sheep. Another 25 percent supports dairy and beef cattle, and 10 percent is used to raise other livestock, such as pigs

Red deer on a commercial deer farm

and red deer. Orchards take 12 percent of the land. The remaining farmland is mostly used to grow specialty items such as flowers or gourmet fruits and vegetables.

About a third of all goods produced are exported. In 1960 half of all exports went to Great Britain. Today 20 percent goes to Australia, 30 percent to Asian countries including Japan, 10 percent to the United States, and only 6.5 percent to Great Britain. Manufactured goods, mostly food and animal products, make up 40 percent of exports. Agricultural-based manufacturing, such as food processing, is the number-one employer in New Zealand. Ninety percent of dairy products are exported, mostly as cheese, butter, and powdered milk.

What New Zealand Grows, Makes, and Mines

Agriculture (1997)

Apples	546,000 metric tons
Barley	377,998 metric tons
Wheat	255,316 metric tons

Manufacturing (1996–1997)

Wood pulp	1,405,300 metric tons
Chemical fertilizers	1,365,000 metric tons
Yarn	21,302 metric tons

Mining (1995)

Limestone	3,930,000 metric tons
Iron ore and sand concentrate	2,362,236 metric tons
Silver	27,800 kilograms

Frozen meat stacked and ready for shipment.

Raw wool is turned into processed wool, wool carpets, and clothing for export. New Zealand is the world's second-largest producer of wool. Frozen meats and leather goods are also important exports. Five percent of exports are fruits, primarily New Zealand's most famous fruit, the kiwi, and the country's many varieties of apples. Wines are the fastest-growing export product.

Kiwifruit

The ancestor of the famous kiwifruit is the Chinese gooseberry. It first came to New Zealand from China as a decorative plant. New Zealand horticulturists have developed new strains that were bigger, tastier, and easier to ship and market. Of course they named the new fuzzy round fruit after their beloved fuzzy round bird, the kiwi.

During the 1980s kiwifruit became hugely popular and profitable for growers. Although kiwifruit is now grown in other countries, New Zealand still grows two-thirds of the world's supply. New Zealand's horticulturists and growers are continuing to develop other fruits suitable for export such as the persimmon, feijoa, nashi pear, and gevuina nuts (similar to macadamia nuts).

Farm Animals

New Zealand is most famous for its 45 million sheep. But the country also raises 5 million beef cattle, 4 million dairy cattle, one and a third million goats, and 1 million deer. No country in the world has a higher farm animal-to-person ratio than New Zealand.

Along with all those sheep, New Zealand is also famous for its remarkable sheepdogs. People come from around the world to watch New Zealand sheepdogs being trained and working to guide sheep. These small dogs respond to whistle and hand signals. They gather, divide, and guide sheep to pasture and back. Their bark warns their human partners of strays and helps find lost sheep. Good dogs are vital in making a sheep ranch successful.

New Zealand sheepdogs at work

Counting Sheep

In 1980 there were 70 million sheep in New Zealand. Recently, however, synthetics such as polypropylene and polyesters have replaced many traditional uses of wool. Because of the end of government subsidies to sheep farms and the declining demand for wool, there are now only about 45 million sheep in the country.

Sheep Talk

As in most businesses, those who work with sheep have their own vocabulary. Today shearing is still done by hand using electric shears. Teams of people, called sheep gangs, work and travel together from farm to farm. Here are some of their slang terms:

Blades—hand shears

Ringer—the fastest shearer in the shearing shed

Gun—a fast shearer

Jingling Johnnies—shearers using hand shears

Gummy—an old toothless sheep

Wigs—short bits of wool from the top of the sheep's head

Smoko—a tea break

Hockey Stick—lamb chop

Hash-me-gandy—sheep-station (farm) stew

There are eight different strains of sheep, each thriving in various parts of the country. They are raised for meat and for wool used in clothing, blankets, carpeting, and other industrial uses. Merino sheep from Australia were the first to arrive, in 1830. They have the finest, softest wool. There are 2.5 million Merinos today, mostly in central Otago on South Island. Romney account for half the sheep in New Zealand. They are especially valued for their meat and coarse wool which makes fine carpets and because they frequently have twins. New Zealand has always been in the forefront of sheep technology: using electric shears, improving breeding and fertility, and developing new uses for wool.

Fishing

As one would expect of an island nation, fishing is an important part of the economy. Indeed, New Zealand's fishing waters are fifteen times that of its landmass. The fishing industry is strictly regulated; there are quotas on the number and size of fish allowed taken. New Zealand is working with the international Marine Stewardship Council to achieve a sustainable and well-managed fishing industry. Only New Zealanders and New Zealand companies are allowed to commercially fish New Zealand waters. However, about half of all com-

A crayfish catch

mercial fishing is done by foreign ships. They either hire New Zealand companies or work in joint ventures with them. New Zealand's rivers and lakes are full of fish, especially the prized brown and rainbow trout. Trout and salmon fishing, swimming with dolphins, and whale watching are being promoted by the tourist industry.

Turning Empty Pastures Into Profits

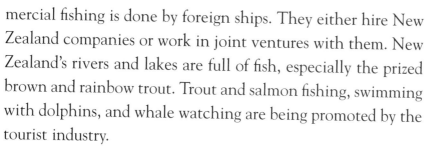

As sheep herd sizes declined, farmers looked for ways to make empty pastureland profitable. Now many farmers are turning their steeper hillside pastures into radiata pine forests for timber. The trees are planted tightly together so they grow very straight with few limbs. After growing for eight years half the

Lumber from radiata pine farms

trees are cut and left on the ground to help prevent erosion and fertilize the soil. In fifteen years, they are harvested and exported to Asia as raw logs, pulp, paper, and lumber. Wood and wood products account for about 5 percent of all exports.

Other farmers are turning their hillside pastures into vineyards. New Zealand's mild climate and good rains produce very successful grapes. During the 1980s some wineries entered their wines in competitions. New Zealand wines quickly and enthusiastically became a worldwide hit, winning many major international awards. Since then, wine production has greatly expanded and is now New Zealand's fastest growing industry. The sloping hills of the Hawkes Bay region of North Island and of the Marlborough region of South Island are considered among the best wine grape-growing areas in the world.

Manufacturing Jobs

In 1997, a quarter of a million people worked in New Zealand's manufacturing industry, 25 percent of them in food processing. About 30 percent helped make machinery or metal products. Ten percent of people worked making clothing and cloth from wool and flax grown in the country and leather from hides raised there. Another 10 percent made wood products. Nine percent made paper products or worked in printing and publishing. Eight percent worked with chemicals, petroleum, coal, rubber, and plastic. And 3 percent worked with concrete, clay, glass, bricks, and plaster. Most manufacturing jobs are in the Auckland area.

Getting Electricity

Although New Zealand has only minor coal and oil reserves, it has other excellent natural energy resources. South Island has several hydro-dams that provide power for South Island and, through an underwater cable, to North Island. North Island also has hydro-dams and is expanding its use of geothermal power. Geothermal power is created in volcanic regions when underground hot lava heats ground-water and creates steampower. There are two natural gas fields, Kapuni and Maui, both on North Island. These provide enough liquefied natural gas for local use and some for exporting. Other potential resources being developed include wind, wave, and solar power.

Geothermal power is a form of natural energy found on North Island.

Overcoming Hard Times

On a world scale, New Zealand now has a good economy, but New Zealanders have worked hard and sacrificed to make it so.

Though the economy boomed after World War II, it faltered in the 1970s. When Great Britain joined the European Community, New Zealand lost its main trading partner. At the same time, fuel prices skyrocketed. New Zealand must import most of its fuel and heavy manufactured goods such as cars. The cost of running a farm and importing and exporting goods soared. So did unemployment. Discouraged, many New Zealanders left the country to find work elsewhere.

To rebuild its flagging economy, the government took several difficult steps. It cut social services, eased rules on industries, ended financial support for farms, and sold some government services, such as the postal and telephone companies, to private owners. They reduced taxes to encourage foreign investment. As tax income fell, the government was forced to borrow money to pay its bills.

By 2000, after reaching a low point three years earlier, the economy was rebounding. Sales were up and unemployment

The Tail of Money

Queen Elizabeth, the official head of government, is on the head side of all New Zealand coins. But the tail side is definitely New Zealand. The tuatara lizard, a Maori-carved tiki face, the kiwi, and Captain Cook's ship, the *Endeavour*, all appear on New Zealand coins. The dollar coin has a kiwi on it and is called the kiwi dollar, or just the kiwi as in "Will you loan me a kiwi, mate?"

New Zealand has no pennies. If something costs $1.01 or $1.02, you pay $1.00. If it costs $1.03 or $1.04, you pay $1.05. This practice of rounding up or down saves people, businesses, banks, and the government from handling and making extra coins. Everyone seems to like the no penny policy.

The New Zealand dollar is worth about U.S. 42 cents and 67 cents Canadian. While many things are priced about the same as they would be in the United States, the exchange rate makes buying New Zealand products and traveling in New Zealand a bargain for Americans. But American goods and travel are expensive for Kiwis.

down. There has been a budget surplus the last few years, but there is still a great deal of national debt to pay off and many services once offered by the government have been suspended. Confidence in the future, however, has returned. The government and the people continue working to improve the economy by encouraging the development of new industries like electronics, telecommunications, and computer software.

Hello, Antarctica!

The first person known to have stepped on the Antarctic continent, in 1895, was seventeen-year-old New Zealander Alexander von Tunzelmann. He was sailing with his uncle, an explorer. Since then, Antarctic exploration, scientific research, and education have been an important part of New Zealand's economy. Christchurch is one of two places in the world that have bases supporting Antarctic research.

The International Antarctic Centre in Christchurch

From the Christchurch research center, scientists fly 12 hours to McMurdo Sound where the United States has a field station—Mac Town. New Zealand's field station, Scott Base, is nearby. Twelve hundred people live at McMurdo Sound, usually for six months at a time. Each year, about 140 flights from Christchurch carry food, mail, supplies, medical and scientific equipment, and replacement personnel to Antarctica. Near the science research center in Christchurch is the Antarctic education center. Its Antarctica simulation room with machine-made snow, wind machines, and 28°F (-2°C) temperature is a favorite of visitors.

Tourism

Tourism is a $4 billion industry and growing. The New Zealand government is heavily promoting tourism, especially in nearby Asian countries. In 1997, more than 1,600,000 visitors came to New Zealand—20 percent came from Japan, another 10 percent from other Asian countries, 29 percent from Australia, and 10 percent from the United States.

New Zealand's diverse environment draws many different kinds of people, but it especially appeals to young adventurers and mature travelers interested in history and nature. Hikers and climbers love its trails and mountains. Hiking is called tramping and trails are called tracks. New Zealand's Milford Track is one of the most famous hiking trails in the world. Adventurers love bungee jumping, skiing, sailing, and white-water rafting. History buffs love learning about the Maori culture. Naturalists love the volcanoes and the plant and animal life.

Tramping the Milford Track

The Economics of Birding

The town of Oamaru on South Island's east coast knows hard times. When the limestone quarry shut down, jobs disappeared. After a few years, people noticed that with the noisy machinery gone, little blue penguins (pictured) began crawling up the seawall and nesting in the crags of the abandoned quarry. Volunteers worked with the Department of Conservation (DOC) to build protected nesting areas, and more penguins came. Each night they climbed out of the ocean and gathered in groups to cross the field to their nests.

Tourists came to watch. Now twenty thousand visitors a year pay to sit in bleachers and watch the little blue penguins come in from the sea while DOC officials lecture about New Zealand's birds and environment. After watching the birds bed down for the night, nearly all the visitors go to Oamaru hotels, restaurants, grocery stores, gas stations, and banks. Because of the little penguins, Oamaru isn't a dying town and times aren't so hard anymore.

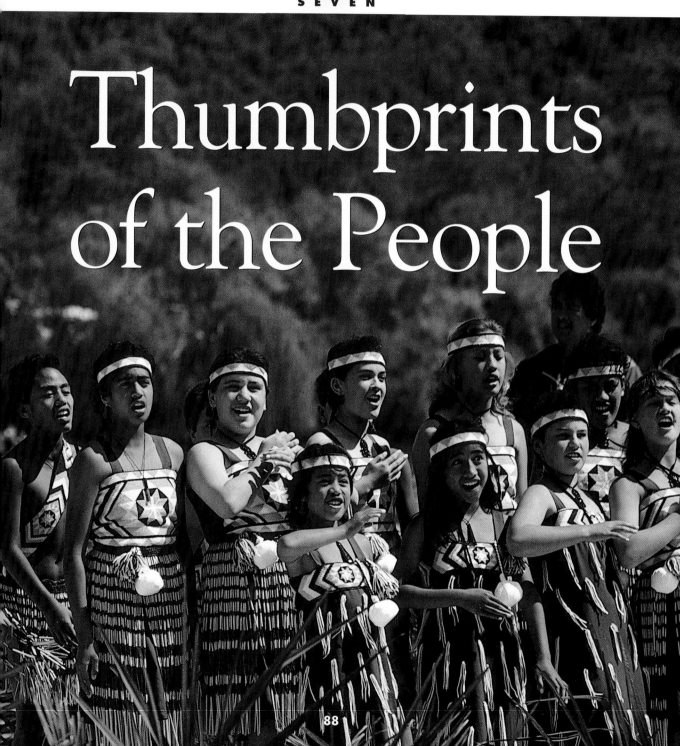

Thumbprints of the People

T HE SYMBOL OF TE PAPA, the new national museum in Wellington, is a human thumbprint. In the Maori tradition thumbprints symbolize that all people are linked together. Because we all have thumbprints, we belong to each other; yet, each person's print is different. This symbolizes that although we are partners in humanity, we still stand alone as unique individuals. This is the philosophy of New Zealand's people. Each person's individualism and ideas are important and must be respected. Yet, they must be balanced with the importance of belonging.

In the days before Europeans, the tribe, the *iwi*, to which one belonged was very important. It still is today, but now people belong to many different kinds of tribes. The Maori belong to their individual tribe. Maori and pakehas both belong to their heritages. They also belong to other "tribes" of school, town, profession, island, and country. New Zealanders are very proud of being Kiwi and of the bicultural heritage of their country. Non-Maori feel connected to Maori traditions because they are part of the culture and history of their country, part of the story of their larger New Zealand tribe.

New Zealanders believe each person is important, but we are partners in humanity.

Ethnic Groups in New Zealand (1996 census)

European	79.6%
Maori	14.5%
Other Polynesian	5.6%
Asian/Indian	5.0%
Other	0.5%

Opposite: **Maori dressed in traditional costumes for a festival**

A young pakeha girl

Pakeha

The largest group of New Zealanders are pakeha, people of European heritage. Pakeha make up about 80 percent of New Zealanders. The majority are of British descent; however, they consider themselves Kiwi, not British. The percentage of pakeha population is much higher on South Island. Most Maori originally settled in the warmer climate of North Island. When the floods of early settlers came, there was unclaimed land on South Island, so many people settled there. South Island remains overwhelmingly pakeha.

Maori and Maoritanga

When Captain Cook sailed around the islands there were about 200,000 Maori. By the 1800s that number was reduced 80 percent because of disease, warfare, and discouragement. Today, more than 450,000 people say they have some

Sharing Breaths

The Maori believe that by sharing breaths, we share lives. This *hongi* greeting is done by touching noses three times so that our breaths and our lives intermingle. This ritual offers our best wishes for a good life and our commitment to each other. An important New Zealand tradition, this greeting is part of many ceremonies.

Maori ancestry. There has been much intermarrying between Maori and pakeha. Maori now live much like pakeha in terms of jobs, homes, and recreational activities. However, most Maori maintain strong ties to their culture.

Maoritanga, Maori culture, hasn't died in history as happened to many other indigenous cultures. It lives because it is cherished. The Maori renaissance of the 1970s rekindled enthusiasm for Maoritanga and highlighted the importance of teaching it to each new generation. Many ancient Maori customs, such as the welcoming dance and the blessing ceremony, have become important parts of New Zealand's cultural personality.

To be Maori is to believe in the sacred, to respect your heritage and traditions, and to honor the land that has sustained Maori for centuries. Maori honor their ancestors and try to follow their ideals. Many Maori trace their ancestry back to one of the original *wakas*, canoes, that carried the first Maori to Aotearoa. They believe their ancestors' spirits mix with the living and offer their knowledge and strength. Their warlike ancestors, they believe, help the Maori win battles today: battles in the courtroom, on the ballfield, on the battlefield, and in the daily individual struggle to build a good life.

Maori children doing a traditional dance

A Maori man

Haere Mai and Kia Ora

Welcome. Greetings. These are two Maori phrases one hears often in New Zealand. But they are more than just phrases. They express the country's values. Haere Mai—Welcome—is how New Zealanders want visitors to feel. This expresses their generous spirit. Kia Ora, like the Hawaiian Aloha, is often used as Hello, Goodbye, and Thank you; but it means much more. Ora comes from the word for breath and relates to the breath of life. By using the greeting Kia Ora, the speaker offers others a wish for a good life.

Speaking in Two Voices

New Zealand has two official languages. The Maori language received official status in 1987. Other than a small number of Samoan and Asian immigrants, everyone speaks English. Maori was on its way to becoming an extinct language spoken mainly by the older generation until the 1970s Maori renaissance. Now it is taught in schools. There are television shows, newscasts, radio stations, and newspapers all in the Maori language. Maori words and place names are commonly used by everyone.

Talking Like a Kiwi

New Zealanders love slang and shortened words. The term Kiwis for New Zealanders started during World War I when New Zealand soldiers went overseas to fight. Kiwis became a quick and affectionate way to distinguish them from the Brits and the Aussies.

Many words are common to all three countries, but here are words you might hear in New Zealand.

bloke, mate – guy

windscreen – windshield

trolley – shopping cart

pudding – dessert (not necessarily pudding at all)

cheers – thank you

crisps – potato chips, or other chips such as taro

busking – performing on the streets for money

good on you – good for you, well-done

trading hours – hours stores are open

dairy – a small grocery store or convenience shop

jumper – sweater

lovely, no worries – it's not a problem

put in the sinbin – being punished or scolded, the penalty box in rugby

mind your step – watch your step

Maori, like other South Sea dialects, is poetic and phonic. The alphabet contains only fourteen letters. In spelling, the only consonants used together are *ng* and *wh*. But vowels often follow vowels. Non-Maori speakers find the language easiest to pronounce if they slow down and remember that each vowel is pronounced. And in every word, each syllable ends in a vowel.

In English, the New Zealand accent is similar to the Australian, however a bit more formal, slightly closer to a British accent. New Zealand uses the British form of English, for example spelling with an *ou* instead of just *o* after consonants and before an *r*—colour, harbour, labour. The *er* at the end of words after *t* is reversed as in theatre and centre.

Population of Major Cities (2001)

Auckland	1,050,000
Wellington	329,000
Christchurch	318,000
Hamilton	153,000
Dunedin	112,000

Eighty percent of New Zealanders have a European heritage.

Population Facts

New Zealand is a young country. Half of the 3.9 million people are under thirty-three. The country's population is growing, but more slowly than in recent history. Increasing immigration adds to population growth. However, the number of people leaving the country to find work elsewhere is also increasing. Overall, the population increases by a person about every 58 minutes—9,000 people a year. The birthrate is slowing as people

Father and son

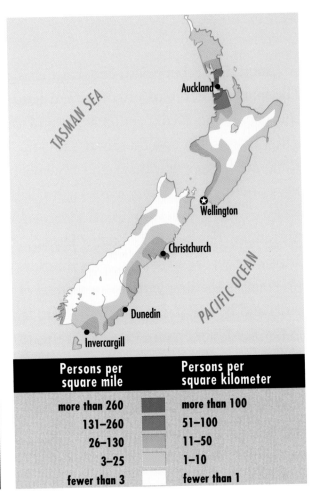

Persons per square mile		Persons per square kilometer
more than 260		more than 100
131–260		51–100
26–130		11–50
3–25		1–10
fewer than 3		fewer than 1

wait longer to get married and start families. The average groom is thirty-one and the average bride twenty-nine. New Zealand is a healthy place to live; the life expectancy is seventy-five for men and eighty for women.

There is plenty of room for those people to move around. The population density at thirty-three people per square mile (thirteen per sq km) is less than half that of the United States. Three-quarters of all New Zealanders live on North Island and half of those live in the Auckland area. Although New

Zealand is predominately an agricultural country only 15 percent of people actually live on farms in rural areas.

New Zealand has a high percentage of immigrants. About 85 percent of its residents were born in New Zealand. The other 15 percent came from other countries. In the 1960s most immigrants came from the British Isles. Now few do. In the 1970s people arrived from the South Sea Islands looking for work. Today there are more Niueans and Cook Islanders in New Zealand than live in those countries. In the 1980s and 1990s the majority of immigrants came from Southeast Asia. Now most are coming from Australia, the United States, Canada, Asia, and the South Sea Islands.

New Zealanders of Asian heritage

A Good Place for a Woman

For women who want to accomplish things, New Zealand is a good place to live. New Zealand's last two prime ministers have been women, Jenny Shipley and Helen Clark. The Maori monarch is a woman, Queen Te Atairangikaahu. For the first time, in 1990, the governor-general who represents Queen Elizabeth is a woman, Dame Catherine Tizard. Women also fill many important and influential positions in business, the arts, professions, education, and industry. In 2000 New Zealand was noted as the ninth-best country for women in the world.

Living in the Godzone

W<small>HEN A</small> K<small>IWI REFERS TO LIVING IN THE</small> "G<small>ODZONE</small>," <small>HE</small> may be talking about both his country and spiritual beliefs. Most New Zealanders say they are a people of faith. One of the things they firmly believe is that their homeland is so amazingly beautiful that not only is it God's best work, it is also where God lives. Many also believe the "Zone" is the best church, and that the best way to be close to God is to be out in the "Zone," fishing or sailing or just admiring God's good work.

The Christian Heritage

The first settlers were Christian missionaries and modern-day Kiwis have inherited those religious affiliations, especially to the Anglican Church (Church of England) and the Roman Catholic Church. About three-fourths of New Zealanders today say they have connections to Christian churches; however, consistent church attendance is rare. Only 3 percent of people attend regularly and those are mostly older people. Although Christianity is the most visible religious philosophy, a fifth of the population claims no religious beliefs at all.

Many areas that were first settled by a particular group still have a predominance of that religion. Christchurch was settled by the Anglican Church of England. The beautiful stone gothic Anglican cathedral in the center of town is one of the most-photographed buildings in New Zealand. It is still the center of religious life for the area. Further south, the

Religions of New Zealand (1996 census)

Anglican (Church of England)	18.0%
Presbyterian	13.0%
Roman Catholic	13.0%
Other Protestant	9.0%
Ratana (Maori)	1.0%
Buddhist	0.8%
Hindu	0.6%
All other religions	8.0%

The Anglican cathedral in Christchurch

towns of Dunedin and Invercargill were established by Scottish settlers. Today, the Presbyterian Church of Scotland remains very important.

As immigrants flow into New Zealand new religions flow in too. Wellington has both a Greek Orthodox Church and a Romanian Orthodox Church. Judaism serves a small percentage of New Zealanders. Immigrants from India brought Muslim and Hindu religions. Hamilton has a Sikh temple and Auckland has an Islamic Center. Southeast Asians brought Buddhism to New Zealand. No matter what religion, New Zealanders have a firm policy of separation of church and state.

For a time the Maori rejected the missionaries' religion. Then, following a few leaders, whole tribes converted together. However, they have interwoven long-held traditions of Maori customs, prophet teachings, and beliefs with Christian teachings and beliefs. They have created their own sense of spirituality. The Ratana and Ringatu churches are Christian churches with a strong Maori influence.

A Maori chapel and flower-covered graves

Like Maori beliefs of old, Maori Christianity is very respectful of its ancestors. Maori graveyards are full of flowers. Leis decorate headstones and bouquets honor those who have passed on, but left their wisdom behind. The main meeting place for Maori ceremonies, the *marae*, honors the ancestors and is designed as a tribute to them. Maori believe that the spirit of the ancestors lives on in the marae, which tell the story of that ancestor's life.

Maori leaving a marae after a baptism

Te Marae

The *marae* is the heart of the Maori world. It is the traditional and sacred meeting place for ceremonies and gatherings, the place for welcoming and celebrating life, for mournful farewells to the dead. It is the place to learn and debate the issues of the country.

The marae consist of several buildings and open areas. The *wharenui* is the main meeting house. It is usually built as a tribute to the ancestors. The building often honors one special ancestor. The wharenui is always open at the back. It is made with a ridge beam and many cross beams—all heavily carved. The carvings tell stories of the ancestor's lives and teachings and really were the first form of Maori writing. The ridge pole represents the backbones of the ancestors. The cross beams represent the ribs. The front flat boards are their open welcoming arms. A dining building is usually nearby. Marae ceremonies, such as the welcome ceremony for visitors, the *powhiri*, are very structured. It is very important to follow customs and tradition carefully to show full respect. To the Maori, actions are as important as words.

The Art of Kiwi Fun

O
NE LONE MAORI WARRIOR STEPS OUT OF THE FOREST, spear in hand, face frightfully contorted. It is lined with curving tattoos. His eyes bulge wide; his tongue hangs low, and his teeth are bared as though he might eat you. With a loud yell he jumps forward into a low crouch and spins his spear. It ends pointing at you.

This is the beginning of a *haka*, a Maori challenge war dance. Rugby teams around the world know the haka well. They also know when they hear that loud threatening warrior cry, they have a battle ahead of them.

Opposite: **Maori carving**

Fierce faces are part of a haka, a Maori war dance.

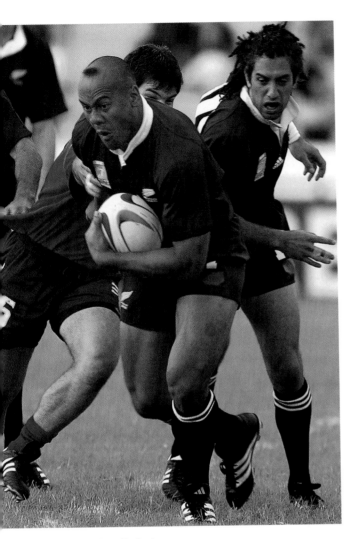

New Zealand's All Blacks playing Argentina in the 2001 Rugby World Cup

Before each game, New Zealand's national rugby team, the All Blacks, challenge the opposing team with a haka. Between the opening intimidation and the All Blacks' extraordinary skill, most often the opposing team goes down in defeat. The All Blacks dominate rugby's international competitions. In this sports-crazed country, nothing is more important than rugby, and no rugby team is more important than the All Blacks. Each member of the All Blacks team is a national hero. Children dream of someday wearing the all-black uniform decorated with the insignia of a New Zealand silver fern. Many top All Blacks players are Maori carrying on the strong warrior tradition of their ancestors.

The All Blacks isn't the only rugby team in New Zealand. There are more than 580 clubs with teams for all ages including senior citizens. Children begin playing on teams at 5 or 6, but by then they usually have been kicking a ball around for years with playmates on the street or backyard. Winning at rugby isn't only for men and boys. In 1998 the national women's rugby team won the Women's World Cup.

Nothing's Better than NZ Sports

If New Zealanders seem fanatical about rugby, it's only natural because they seem to love all sports. After all, if you're in New Zealand, what could be better than being out on the Bay of Islands on a sparkling day, trimming your sail to catch the gentle breeze? Unless it's being on the Marlborough Sounds on a stormy day raising the spinnaker sail to tame the wild sea. Unless it's climbing the mountain crest and seeing the first rays of the new day shine on the South Pacific Ocean. Or walking the Milford Track and seeing the morning sun turn the dewy forest silver. Or lying on your surfboard waiting for the perfect wave to roll in from the Tasman Sea.

Some people believe nothing is better than galloping along the surf's edge. Or meeting your mates for cricket, or

A gallop along the beach

Kayaking with orcas

rugby, or lawn bowls. Or paddling your kayak alongside surfacing dolphins. Or feeling your fishing pole yank as the big one strikes. Or flying like a bird on the upswing of a bungee jump. Or scuba diving among fish so thick and colorful you might be swimming through a rainbow in the sky. Or maybe jogging along the roadway admiring all the neighbors' gardens. Really, what could be better than sports in New Zealand? Unless it's soaking in a natural hot spring to ease your exhausted muscles afterward.

New Zealand is known around the world for great sports and great athletes. In world competitions Kiwis are formidable opponents and often gallant winners. Rarely do the Olympic Games go by without some Kiwi winning a gold medal. Peter Snell and John Walker set records and won Olympic medals in mid-distance running. New Zealand's canoeing and rowing teams have won several Olympic medals. Mark Todd and Blyth Tait and their horses have won equestrian medals. Brother and sister Bruce and Barbara Kendall have both won sail-boarding medals. Beatrice Faumuina took the discus gold in the World Track and Field Championships. Women's netball, similar to basketball, is very popular, and New Zealand and Australia seem to trade the world championship back and forth. Known for their guts, grit, and ability to keep going, the New Zealand team routinely wins the world extreme eco-race challenge. Sir Peter Blake won the Whitbread Round-the-World solo yacht race before he began captaining the New Zealand entry in the America's Cup race.

Bronze medalist Barbara Kendall (right) at the 2000 Summer Olympics

New Zealand has more golf courses for its size population than any other country and great golfers to play on them. One of the world's largest "fun runs" with more than 70,000 participants takes place along the Auckland waterfront. But that's fitting since New Zealander Arthur Lydiard is considered the inventor of jogging. And the world owes the thrill of bungee jumping to its inventor, New Zealander A. J. Hackett. However, in a country known for challenging thrill sports, the biggest annual sporting event is the lawn bowls national championships.

Sir Edmund Hillary (1919–)

As a child he loved hiking and climbing Auckland's hills and volcano cones. As an adult, he moved to bigger things. He dreamed of finding a route to the top of Nepal's Mount Everest, the world's highest peak at 29,028 feet (8,848 m). No one had ever succeeded in climbing it before. By 1953, Hillary had twice tried and twice failed. But in true Kiwi spirit, he persevered. Finally, on May 29, he and his climbing partner, Nepalese Sherpa Tenzing Norgay, successfully made it to the top of Everest and to the height of fame.

Afterward many mountaineers dreamed of climbing Everest. Today, the mountain is cluttered and tamed by thousands of feet of fixed ropes in difficult places and sixty aluminum ladders on ice falls. Hillary commented, "I feel lucky to have been up there climbing when it was a different sort of mountaineering." He has written several books about his climbing experiences.

After conquering Everest, Hillary continued climbing and doing important high-altitude scientific research.

He and his crew became the first people to reach the South Pole since Scott, forty-five years earlier.

In Nepal Hillary became very fond of the Sherpa people and has helped establish schools and medical facilities for them. In New Zealand, he has lent his name to a national organization promoting outdoor activities and sports for young people. New Zealanders, in 1996, voted Hillary as the person who best displayed the spirit of New Zealand. Today Hillary is pictured on the $5 bill.

Black Magic *Does It*

In this country full of "yachties," sailing is second only to rugby as the national passion. In Auckland, nicknamed the City of Sails, an average of one of every four households owns a boat. With so many boats, Kiwis love a good race, and no race is better than the America's Cup.

This "world series" of yacht racing began in 1851 as the Louis Vuitton Cup. Since then, it has been so consistently won by the United States that it has become known as the America's Cup. In this race all challengers compete for the right to race against the previous Cup winner. Now the winning challenger is awarded the Louis Vuitton Cup.

In 1995 New Zealand's boat *Black Magic*, captained by Peter Blake and Russell Coutts, won the Cup. There was hardly a prouder moment in New Zealand sporting history. In 2000 it was New Zealand's turn to defend ownership of the Cup. Over several months the best yachts and racing teams from around the world competed on the Hauraki Gulf out of Auckland. Italy's *Pravda* won the right to sail against New Zealand's *Black Magic*. *Pravda* and the sleek *Black Magic* sailed against each other in nine series of races. By the end of the three weeks the whole world saw that the Kiwis knew their way around wind and waves. *Black Magic* did it again! The Cup, for the first time, went to a repeat winner other than the United States. New Zealanders brimmed with pride and celebrations filled the streets and bays around the country. Perhaps some day the America's Cup will become known as the Kiwi Cup.

New Zealand (in front) winning the America's Cup in 2000

The Art of Design

For a country well-known as excelling in sports, it may surprise some to learn that New Zealanders also excel in art and design.

Kiwi art graces New Zealand products such as hand-painted pottery, business and sports clothing, linens, yacht designs, and furniture. Designs are often elegant, but more often, delightfully charming. Maori symbols are a favorite way to show the Kiwi character. Occasionally, they are used in surprising places, such as the design on streets grates and sidewalk flower pots.

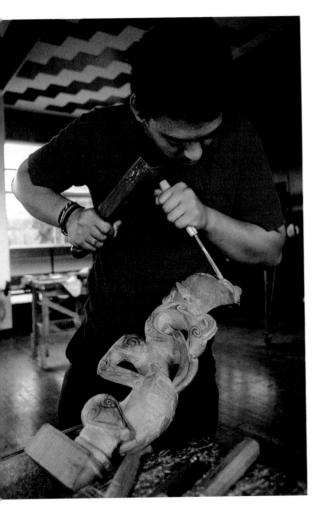

Wood carving is a traditional Maori skill.

Murals, paintings, and sculptures make New Zealand's city streets a delight to walk. All the arts enjoy wide support. Nelson sponsors a wearable-art festival. Wellington sponsors the New Zealand International Festival of the Arts. This artistic environment produces great artists such as painters Frances Hodgkins and Colin McCahon.

The renovated downtown waterfront area of Wellington is a treasure of contemporary architecture and design with a Maori influence. Here in the heart of the city, the arts have made everything beat faster. The new Te Papa indoor and outdoor museum, the City to Sea Bridge, the brick walkways patterned after Maori weavings, and the town square all reflect New Zealand's commitment to move forward, with its Aotearoa past intact.

Maori carving is one of the skills moving from the past to the future. Traditionally, the

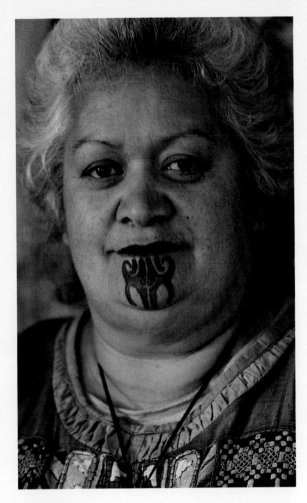

The Art of Maori Tattoos

Captain Cook's crew were most impressed when they saw the *moko*—tattoos of curving lines—on the faces and thighs of the Maori. These were actually carved into the skin. The elaborate designs of moko made the warrior look very fierce. The more moko a person had, the braver warrior he was thought to be. Women also had tattoos, but usually on their lips and chin.

Making these tattoos was a long and painful process. First lines were traced on the skin with charcoal. Then the moko expert would carve grooves into the skin and pound pigment into the grooves with a toothed chisel. Only a small area could be done at a time and it often led to swelling and sometimes infection. Today most Maori don't get tattooed, though many do wear temporary tattoos for special tribal events.

carvings were a form of written language, telling stories and histories through pictures. Using greenstone tools carvers fashioned large items such as war canoes and small items such as amulets and fish hooks from greenstone, bone, and wood. Greenstone is a type of jade found on South Island in the Otago region.

Entertaining the World

In recent years Kiwi entertainers have exploded onto the world scene. The film industry has received attention because of several new directors and their unique films. Most noted is the Academy Award-winning movie *The Piano*, by New Zealand director and playwright Jane Champion. Not only was the movie filmed in New Zealand, many local actors participated in it, including Anna Paquin age eleven, who won the Academy Award for best supporting actress. Other recent acclaimed films by Kiwi directors include *Map of the Human Heart*, *Once Were Warriors* (with an all-Maori cast), and its sequel, *What Becomes of the Broken-Hearted*.

People from around the world may have enjoyed watching New Zealand scenery without even realizing it.

Anna Paquin

Several popular television shows have been filmed in New Zealand, among them *Hercules*, *Cleopatra 2525*, *Jack of All Trades*, and *Xena: Warrior Princess*, starring New Zealander Lucy Lawless.

New Zealanders enjoy music of all kinds. They have an outstanding Royal Ballet, the New Zealand Symphony Orchestra, and the National Opera, with stars such as Dame Kiri Te Kanawa. Music performances comes in all flavors including Maori drums and jazz festivals at Nelson and the Bay of Islands. The World Busker's Festival at Christchurch celebrates street performers, and Dunedin rocks with youth music at the university.

First among the famous New Zealand writers is Wellington's Katherine Mansfield who is considered one of the most important creators of the modern short story. She has been followed by several great writers including Janet Frame, Keri Hulme, who won the Booker Prize for her novel *The Bone People*, and famed children's writer Margaret Mahy.

A concert performance in Wellington

Russell Crowe

Movie superstar Russell Crowe was born in Wellington on April 7, 1964. He is one-eighth Maori. His parents, who catered food for television and movie sets in New Zealand and Australia, often took Russell along. Soon young Russell was in front of the cameras as an extra. At 16, he and friends formed the band 30 Odd Foot of Grunts. The band still records, and Crowe still sings and plays guitar with them.

Crowe first found work as an actor in Australian soap operas and then moved to low-budget movies. His movies became bigger and better, but his fame did not until he was cast in *L.A. Confidential*, an Academy Award-winning movie. After that came the lead role in *Gladiator* for which he won an Academy Award for best actor. By the time he was filming *Proof of Life* he was a worldwide superstar. Crowe still considers Australia and New Zealand home. He even refuses to drink French wines in order to protest France's nuclear testing. He credits his success to his strong work ethic.

Te Papa (Our Place)

New Zealand has a great new national cultural and historical treasure, the Te Papa Museum in Wellington. It's one of the most modern and unusual interactive museums in the world. The museum follows New Zealand's geological, biological, and human history. It celebrates individuals and cultures important to New Zealand. A special exhibit explains the historical Treaty of Waitangi that founded the nation. Industries and artifacts of old and modern New Zealand are on display. And it houses some of the country's finest artwork. It's outdoor gardens, Bush City, represent the natural vegetation of the nation and contain fossils, moa bones, rocks, and caves.

The museum designers have used technology to teach. An earthquake house shakes up museum visitors like a real earthquake might. It has movies, interactive displays, learning centers, a real marae used for ceremonies, a new war canoe, and even amusement-park-style activities and games. A computerized life-sized plastic sheep tests your shearing ability. People especially love the simulators, which take them through time warps to New Zealand's past, flying over the Southern Alps, or skiing on a volcano.

To make sure that the museum continues to belong to all people, continues to be "Our Place," the directors have decided not to charge admission so that everyone may come in anytime (between 9 and 5).

Growing Up Kiwi

TODAY, GROWING UP KIWI MEANS BEING PART OF A COMMunity that appreciates the contributions of many cultures, backgrounds, and experiences. It means growing up knowing the joy of outdoor fun and knowing how to work hard. It means reaching for wide horizons through education. It means belonging to a special group of people in a special land.

Opposite: **Taking time for fun**

Widening horizons in a classroom

National Holidays in New Zealand

New Year's Day	January 1
Waitangi Day	February 6
Good Friday/Easter Monday	March or April
ANZAC Day	April 25
Queen's Birthday	First Monday in June
Labor Day	Fourth Monday in October
Christmas Day	December 25
Boxing Day	December 26

School Year Round

New Zealanders have found that frequent vacations keep students fresh and more enthusiastic. To accomplish this, the school year is divided into four terms, with vacations in between that last from two to six weeks. The four divisions are late January to mid-April; April until the beginning of July; mid-July until late in September; and mid-October to December.

Perhaps Kiwis have a chance to excel at sports more than many countries because life here isn't as rushed as in most Western countries. People take time for fun. Stores are rarely open past six in the evening, even the largest stores in Auckland. Restaurants shut down around nine at night. People don't let business control their lives. If it is a fine windy day, they plan a sail. On a fine day with flat wind, they plan a beach picnic.

Learning in New Zealand

New Zealanders believe that providing quality education assures a good future for the country. The education act passed in 1877 guarantees a free education for all. Children usually attend school from ages five to nineteen. At age three many children go to preschool, including Maori language and culture school. The school years are divided into levels numbered by years, sometimes called forms. Most students start primary school on their fifth birthday and study there until they are eleven. They go into intermediate school years seven and eight and to secondary school for years nine to thirteen.

The school curriculum reflects New Zealand's bicultural heritage and concentrates on seven main areas: language, mathematics, science, technology, social sciences, art, and physical well-being. Attitudes, values, and socials skills are also taught. There are optional programs such as same sex secondary schools, adult learning programs, and Maori-language immersion programs. Integrated schools emphasizing particular philosophies are private, though they receive some government funding. Correspondence schools broadcast lessons for students being home-schooled in rural areas. Some schools require their students to wear uniforms.

Students can earn any of three types of graduation certificates. To get a school certificate, students must pass a national test at the end of their eleventh year. To earn their sixth form certificate they must pass

Farm children being home-schooled

Students wearing school uniforms

national tests in each subject after year twelve. Higher school certificates are awarded to those completing year thirteen. Students then take college entrance exams. Those with high scores receive scholarships. There are eight major universities and many trade schools in New Zealand.

Traveling and the O.E.

Like the ancient Polynesian sailors, today's Kiwis are great travelers. They love traversing their country roads in small campers called caravans. To accommodate travelers on budgets, nearly all towns and recreational areas have several inexpensive hostels. When they can, Kiwis head off to nearby Australia, or Southeast Asia, or Polynesia, or any exciting place beyond the horizon.

After finishing their studies, many young people take several months to work and travel around the world experiencing new cultures. They call this "doing an O.E.," an overseas experience. Many start in Australia or England where cultural ties are strong and they can get work permits. From there they may travel to continental Europe. Those who can afford it head for the United States, Canada, and Mexico. Many teach English in Asia. When they return to New Zealand it is with a new understanding of the world and its people.

On the Road

Like much of the world, New Zealanders drive on the left side of the road. In urban areas a popular type of intersection is the roundabout. All roads enter the circular intersection like

New Zealanders drive on the left side of the road.

spokes going to the center of a wheel. Cars drive around the circle until they reach the exiting road they want. If they miss it, they circle again.

Except in major cities during rush hour, traffic jams (called tail-backs) are not a problem. Superfreeways do not exist beyond the outskirts of Auckland. Almost all the roads that

A small car ferry

connect city to city are two-lane country roads with a maximum speed limit of 60 mph (100 kph). Many country bridges are one lane. Road travel takes much longer than in North America. Much of the mountainous country on South Island has no roads for cars. Large ferries run between North Island and South Island.

Living in Town

About 80 percent of New Zealanders live in towns. Each of New Zealand's towns has a distinctive personality. In the historical far north, communities have a tropical feel. However, Auckland is a true cosmopolitan city with over a million people. It has skyscrapers, heavy traffic, and public areas with gardens and sculptures. At major intersections, all cars stop together, and people wearing business black and talking on cell phones cross any way they wish, even diagonally. Wellington is a sophisticated, multi-cultural city, home to the New Zealand symphony and the Royal New Zealand Ballet. Because of its Victorian homes and hills, it is often called Little San Francisco in the South Pacific.

Christchurch, established by the Anglican English, is the commercial center of South Island. The neo-Gothic Church of England Cathedral, Botanical Gardens, and Avon River

The Botanical Gardens in Christchurch

The University of Otago
in Dunedin

give Christchurch the most English feel of New Zealand's towns. It is nicknamed the Garden City. Dunedin (Du-ne-din) remains a bit distanced from the rest of the country. It was settled by the Scottish church and is strongly influenced by its heritage. Dunedin is Gaelic for Edinburgh. Perhaps because of the University of Otago's presence, Dunedin has become a center of influence on the world's popular music scene. The lakeside city of Queenstown has become an international destination for adventurous sport. Bungee jumping was invented here. President Clinton vacationed in Queenstown in 1998.

Eating in New Zealand

When people around the world talk about great cuisines they usually mention French, Italian, and Thai. But lately some are adding New Zealand to the list. Historically, New Zealanders ate a rather bland English diet that featured meat, usually lamb, boiled potatoes, and peas. In the last decade, immigrants have begun to influence New Zealand food. The new style of cooking is called Pacific Fusion. It combines the solid European menu with fresh foods and spices common to the Pacific Islands and Southeast Asia.

Fresh foods are used whenever possible, and cooked quickly to keep their color and crunch. Previously, a piece of white fish would have been baked in a buttered pan and overcooked. Now it might be coated with flour made of hazelnuts and quickly sautéed. It might be topped with a salsa of diced kiwi, strawberries, and papaya, mixed with chopped Asian

Dining outdoors on a beautiful New Zealand day

lemongrass and sweet basil. Instead of being accompanied by New Zealand's traditional kumara or pumpkin soup, it might be served with a Thai curried pumpkin soup. If it sounds as if New Zealanders eat well, they certainly do. An international study of food availability, quality, quantity, and variety found that New Zealanders are the best-fed people in the world.

Looking to the Future

New Zealand has problems common to all countries: the fight to give young people direction and purpose in the world, the

The Maori Hangi

The Maori hangi is the traditional method of cooking a feast in an underground oven (*umu*). It is still used today for special occasions and cultural events. A hangi meal includes meat such as lamb, chicken, and pork; potatoes and kumara sweet potatoes; vegetable pieces such as cabbage, onions, and carrots; and steamed bread pudding or custard.

Hangis take time to prepare. Six hours before eating, the cooks light logs topped with volcanic rocks in a shallow pit in the ground. As the fire burns out, they wrap the food tightly in foil packets and put the packets in a steel basket: meat on the bottom, pudding on the top. The basket is placed on top of the white-hot rocks and covered with soaking-wet sheets and towels. A potato placed between the towels lets the chef check to see if the hangi is fully cooked. The basket and towels are covered with dirt so that no steam escapes. After about three hours the food should be ready to eat. They carefully remove the dirt, check the potato, and take out the basket of food—a traditional Maori meal cooked in the ground. Hangis are best enjoyed with lots of friends and family.

fight to preserve the environment in an increasingly polluted world, the fight to keep moving the country forward intellectually and economically. It also has unique problems: living up to the Treaty of Waitangi and making restitution for land and forests and fishing rights improperly taken from the Maori. They want to do this without destroying the rights of new owners who bought their land in good faith or disturbing the areas of land, such as national parks, belonging to all New Zealanders.

But overall, life in New Zealand is good. New Zealand is blessed with an abundance of natural resources and a well-educated population. But best of all is that Kiwi sense of fun and sly sense of humor. After all, not every country can get away with telling visitors to "Go jump off a cliff," then charging them money to do so. As they say in New Zealand, "*Kia Ora* and see you later, mate."

Timeline

New Zealand History

Polynesian people arrive in New Zealand and call the area Aotearoa.	About A.D. 1000
Dutch explorer Abel Tasman sails along the west coast of Aotearoa's South Island.	1642
Other Dutch explorers name Aotearoa's islands Nieuw Zeeland.	1643
Captain James Cook claims New Zealand for England.	1769
Missionaries from Australia arrive in New Zealand to bring Christianity to the Maori.	1814
The Treaty of Waitangi is signed making Britain the governing force in New Zealand.	1840
England gives New Zealand a constitution and the right to govern itself.	1852
The Maori form a government parallel to that of the British-controlled government and elect a chief to unite the Maori tribes.	1858

World History

2500 B.C.	Egyptians build the Pyramids and the Sphinx in Giza.
563 B.C.	The Buddha is born in India.
A.D. 313	The Roman emperor Constantine recognizes Christianity.
610	The Prophet Muhammad begins preaching a new religion called Islam.
1054	The Eastern (Orthodox) and Western (Roman) Churches break apart.
1066	William the Conqueror defeats the English in the Battle of Hastings.
1095	Pope Urban II proclaims the First Crusade.
1215	King John seals the Magna Carta.
1300s	The Renaissance begins in Italy.
1347	The Black Death sweeps through Europe.
1453	Ottoman Turks capture Constantinople, conquering the Byzantine Empire.
1492	Columbus arrives in North America.
1500s	The Reformation leads to the birth of Protestantism.
1776	The Declaration of Independence is signed.
1789	The French Revolution begins.

New Zealand History

The Land Wars take place as Maori lose land in unfair land deals.	1860–1872
England gives New Zealand the right to establish its own representative government.	1865
Maori men are given the right to vote and given four seats in Parliament.	1867
New Zealand becomes the first country in the world to give women the right to vote.	1893
New Zealand becomes a dominion, a self-governing country, within the British Empire.	1907
About 100,000 soldiers from New Zealand help the Allies in World War I.	1914–1918
About 140,000 New Zealanders, including Maori, help the Allies in World War II.	1939–1945
New Zealand becomes an independent member of the British Commonwealth of Nations.	1947
New Zealander Edmund Hillary and his Sherpa climbing partner Tenzing Norgay are the first people to reach the top of Mount Everest in Nepal.	1953
Queen Te Atairangikaahu becomes the first female monarch of the Maori.	1966
New Zealand's currency changes from the New Zealand pound to the New Zealand dollar.	1967
Young Maori begin a movement to reclaim Maori culture.	1970s
The Waitangi Tribunal is established to handle Maori land claims.	1975
New Zealand's government declares the country a nuclear-free zone.	1985
Maori joins English as an official language in New Zealand.	1987
A yachting team from New Zealand wins the America's Cup.	1995
Jenny Shipley becomes the first female prime minister of New Zealand.	1997
New Zealand again wins the America's Cup.	2000

World History

1865	The American Civil War ends.
1914	World War I breaks out.
1917	The Bolshevik Revolution brings communism to Russia.
1929	Worldwide economic depression begins.
1939	World War II begins, following the German invasion of Poland.
1945	World War II ends.
1957	The Vietnam War starts.
1969	Humans land on the moon.
1975	The Vietnam War ends.
1979	Soviet Union invades Afghanistan.
1983	Drought and famine in Africa.
1989	The Berlin Wall is torn down, as communism crumbles in Eastern Europe.
1991	Soviet Union breaks into separate states.
1992	Bill Clinton is elected U.S. president.
2000	George W. Bush is elected U.S. president.

Fast Facts

Official name: New Zealand (English); Aotearoa (Maori)

Capital: Wellington

Official languages: English, Maori

Official religion: None

Auckland

New Zealand's flag

The Milford Track

Year of founding:	1840
National anthems:	"God Defend New Zealand" and "God Save the Queen"
Government:	Constitutional monarch with one legislative house
Chief of state:	British monarch, represented by a governor-general
Head of government:	Prime minister
Area and dimensions:	104,454 square miles (270,534 sq km)
Greatest distance north to south:	1,000 miles (1,610 km)
Greatest distance east to west:	250 miles (402 km)
Latitude and longitude of geographic center:	41° S, 174° E
Land and water borders:	West—Tasman Sea, East—the South Pacific Ocean
Highest elevation:	Mount Cook, 12,349 feet (3,764 m) above sea level
Lowest elevation:	Sea level along the coast
Average temperature extremes:	85°F (29°C) in January; 35°F (2°C) in July
Greatest annual precipitation:	473 inches (1,200 cm) on the western part of South Island
Lowest annual precipitation:	11 inches (28 cm) on the eastern part of South Island
National population (2001):	3,864,000

International Antarctic Centre

Population of major cities (2001):

Auckland	1,050,000
Wellington	329,000
Christchurch	318,000
Hamilton	153,000
Dunedin	112,000

Famous landmarks:

- ▶ *Auckland Harbor*
- ▶ *Fox Glacier and Franz Josef Glacier* in Westland National Park on South Island
- ▶ *International Antarctic Centre*, Christchurch, South Island
- ▶ *Marlborough Sounds*, northern tip of South Island
- ▶ *Milford Track* in Fjordland National Park on South Island
- ▶ *Otago Early Settlers Museum*, Dunedin, South Island
- ▶ *Pohutu*, in Whakarewarewa geyser area on North Island
- ▶ *Te Papa Museum*, Wellington, North Island
- ▶ *Waipoua Kauri Forest* on North Island
- ▶ *Waitangi Treaty House* on North Island

Industry: Trade, manufacturing, and tourism are New Zealand's leading industries. Wool and processed foods such as butter, cheese, dried-milk products, and lamb meat are New Zealand's main exports. Important manufactured goods include chemicals, iron and steel, oil products, textiles, and wood products. Tourism, in U.S. dollars, is about a $2 billion business each year.

Currency: The New Zealand dollar (NZ$) is the basic unit of money, with 100 cents to one dollar. In July 2001, 1 NZ$ equaled $0.41 in U.S. currency.

Currency

Maori children

System of weights and measures:	Metric	
Literacy rate:	Near 100 percent	

Common Maori words and phrases:

Ae	Yes
Awhi	Help
Haere mai.	Welcome.
Haere ra.	Farewell, good-bye.
kai	food, eat, dine
Kei te pehea koe?	How are you? (to one person)
Tena koe	Hello (to one person)
Tena koru	Hello (to two people)
wai	water

Famous People:

Jane Campion	(1955–)
Movie director and playwright	
Sir Edmund Hillary	(1919–)
Mountain climber	
Keri Hulme	(1947–)
Author	
Katherine Mansfield	(1888–1923)
Author	
Colin McCahon	(1919–1987)
Artist	
Sir Apirana Ngata	(1874–1950)
Political leader	
Ernest Rutherford	(1871–1937)
Scientist	
Jenny Shipley	(1997–1999)
First female prime minister (years in office)	
Dame Kiri Te Kanawa	(1944–)
Opera singer	
Queen Te Atairangikaahu	(1931–)
Maori leader	

Queen Te Arairangikaahu

To Find Out More

Nonfiction

▶ Ball, John. *We Live in New Zealand*. New York: Bookwright Press, 1982.

▶ Macdonald, Robert. *Maori*. New York: Thomson Learning, 1994.

▶ Mahy, Margaret. *My Mysterious World*. New York: Richard C. Owen Publishers, 1995.

▶ Orbell, Margaret. *Maori Folktales in Maori and English*. London: C. Hurst & Co., 1968.

▶ Osborne, Christine. *Australian and New Zealand Food and Drink*. New York: Bookwright Press, 1989.

▶ Stewart, Whitney. *Sir Edmund Hillary: To Everest and Beyond*. Minneapolis: Lerner Publications, 1996.

▶ Vernon, Adele. *The Hoiho: New Zealand's Yellow-Eyed Penguin*. New York: Putnam, 1991.

▶ Wiremu, Graham. *The Maoris of New Zealand*. Vero Beach, FL: Rourke Publications, 1989.

Fiction

▶ Mahy, Margaret. *Underrunners*. New York: Viking, 1992.

▶ Savage, Deborah. *A Stranger Calls Me Home*. Boston: Houghton Mifflin, 1992.

Web sites

▶ **New Zealand Embassy**
www.nzemb.org/backgrounder
Information about New Zealand from its embassy in the United States. Many links available and places to contact for more information.

▶ **Gateway to New Zealand Government**
www.govt.nz
Official government of New Zealand site links to all departments and people to contact for more information.

▶ **New Zealand Tourism**
www.purenz.com
Official tourism site.

▶ **Maori Culture**
www.maori.culture.co.nz
Extensive site of Maori culture and history. Many links and downloadable music, art, etc., in both Maori and English.

▶ **Te Papa Museum**
www.tepapa.govt.nz
Official site of the new national museum.

▶ **International Antarctic Centre**
www.iceberg.co.nz
Official site of New Zealand's Antarctic research and education.

▶ **NZ Herald Newspaper**
www.nzherald.co.nz
Site of the main newspaper for Auckland and New Zealand.

Videos

▶ *New Zealand: Islands of Adventure.* London: International Video Network, 1994.

▶ *Touring New Zealand.* Chicago: Questar Inc., 1998.

Organizations and Embassies

▶ **New Zealand Embassy**
37 Observatory Circle, NW
Washington, DC 20008

▶ **New Zealand Consulate**
12400 Wilshire Blvd., Suite 1150
Los Angeles, CA 90025

Index

Page numbers in *italics* indicate illustrations.

A

agriculture, 47, 53, 54–55, 57, 61, 75–78
albatross, *30*
All Blacks, 104, *104*
America's Cup, 108–109, *109*
Anglican cathedral, 98
Antarctica, 85–86
ANZAC Day, 56
Aotearoa, 11–12
art and design, *102*, 109–112
Auckland, 25, 122–123

B

Batten, Jean, 56, *56*
beach, *116*
Beehive, *67*, 73
bicycles, 120
birds, *30*, *31*, 31–34
birdwatching, 87
Black Magic, 109, *109*
Blake, Sir Peter, 107, 109
Botanical Gardens, *123*
Bracken, Thomas, 72
British colonization, 49–55
bungee jumping, 9, *9*, 13, 125

C

Canterbury Plains, 26
car ferry, *122*
Champion, Jane, 112
Christchurch, 25, 123, 125
Christianity, 97–98, 99–100
Church of the Good Shepherd, *96*
Clark, Helen, 69, *69*
classroom, *117*
climate, 12, 26, 27–28
Cook, James, 32, 45, *45*, 46
Coutts, Russell, 109
Crowe, Russell, 115, *115*
cuisine, 125–126, 127
culture, 55
    art and design, 109–112
    cuisine, 125–126, 127
    entertainment industry, 112–113, 115
    languages, 63, 92–93
    lifestyle, 117–118
    literature, 114
    Maoritanga, 91, 99–101
    Maori tattoos, 111, *111*
    music, 114, *114*
    philosophy, 89
    preservation and awareness, 57–58

sharing breaths, 90, *90*
sports, 104–109
war dance (haka), 103, *103*
currency, 60, 84, *84*, *85*

D

Department of Conservation, 87
Dunedin, 125

E

earthquakes, 21, 22
economy, 13, 55, 75–87
  after World War II, 57
  stock exchange, 20
education, 118–120
electricity, 83. *See also*
  hydroelectric power
Elizabeth, Queen, 64, *64*
Ellerslie, 12–13
entertainment industry, 112–113, 115
environmental concerns, 13, 32, 58–59
exports, 76–77, *77*, 82

F

farming, 47, 53, 54–55, 57, 61, 75–78
Faumuina, Beatrice, 107
fern trees, *40*, 41
fishing, 81, *81*
food, 125–126, 127
forests, 40, 81–82
Frame, Janet, 114

G

geography, 16–19
  earthquakes, 21, 22
  mountains, 15–16, 22–24, *24*, 26
  North Island, 20–21
  rivers and lakes, 19, 21
  South Island, 22–26
  tectonic plates, 15
  volcanoes, 15, 21, 22
geothermal mud pool, *16*
geothermal power, 83, *83*
giant sea squid, 39
glowworms, 37, *37*
Godzone, 97
gold, 52
Gondwanaland, 31
government, 63–66
  capital, 71, 73
  court system, 70
  executive, 68–69
  local, 73
  office buildings, *63*
  ombudsmen, 70–71
  Parliament, 66–67
  political parties, 68
gravitational pull, 28
Greenpeace, 59
greenstone, 112
Grey, George, 54

H

Hackett, A. J., 107
Hawkes Bay vineyard, *74*
Hillary, Sir Edmund, 56, 108, *108*

Hobson, William, 49–50, 51
Hone Heke, Chief, 54
horseback riding, *105*
Hulme, Keri, 114
human rights, 58
hydro-dams, 83
hydroelectric power, 19, 59, 83

I

immigration, 95
independence, 55, 60
insects, 34, 35, *35*
International Antarctic Centre, 86, *86*
irrigation, 19

K

kauri tree, 41, *41*
kayaking with orcas, *106*
kea (mountain parrot), 33, *33*, 34
Kendall, Barbara, 107, *107*
Kendall, Bruce, 107
King Movement, 52
kiwi bird, 12, *12*, 33–34
kiwifruit, 78, *78*
Kupe (Polynesian navigator), 11

L

Lake Rotomahana, 22
lakes. *See* rivers and lakes
land grabs, 48, 50
land wars, 50–54
languages, 63, 92–93
Lawless, Lucy, *113*

lawlessness, 46–47, 49
literature, 114
livestock, 53, 54–55, 75–76, 78–80, *79*
Louis Vuitton Cup, 108–109, *109*
lumber industry, 81–82, *82*
Lydiard, Arthur, 107

M

Mahy, Margaret, 114
Mansfield, Katherine, 114
manufacturing, 25, 76–77, 82–83
Manukau, 25
Maori, 11, *11*, 43–44, 48, 88, 89, 91
    carving, *102*
    chapel, *99*
    culture, 90–91, 99–101
    hangi, *127*
maps
    early Maori population, *43*
    European exploration, *45*
    European settlement, *49*
    geographical, *17*
    geopolitical, *10*
    national parks, *27*
    Pacific Ring of Fire, *22*
    political divisions, *73*
    population density, *94*
    resource, *75*
    tectonic plates, *22*
    Wellington, *71*
marine life, 38, 38–39, *39*
Marsden, Samuel, 47, 48
metric system, 86
Milford Sound, 8, 22, *23*
Milford Track, 87, *87*

military troops, *57, 61*
mining, 77
missionaries, 47–49
moa bird, 33, *33*
money, 60, 84, *84*, 85
mountains, 15–16, 22–24, *24*, 26
Mount Cook National Park, *24*
Mount Ruapehu, *21*
Mount Tarawera, 22
museums, 89, 115
music, 114, *114*

N

national holidays, 118
national parks, 26–27
national symbols
    anthem, 72
    flag, 72, *72*
    kiwi bird, 12, *12*
natural resources, 26, 83
    gold, 52
New Zealand Wars, 50–54
Norgay, Tenzing, 108
North Island, *14*, 18, *18*, 20–21
North Shore, 25
nuclear testing, 59

O

office buildings, *71*
ombudsmen, 70–71
Otago Plateau, 26
Otuataua Stonefields, 25
outdoor restaurant, *126*

P

Pacific Fusion, 125–126
Pancake Rocks, *15*
Paquin, Anna, 112, *112*
Parliament buildings, *67*
penguins, 38, *38*, 87, *87*
people, *94*, *95*. *See also* Maori
    British, 49–55
    ethnic groups, 89
    European, 44–47, 49–55
    European explorers, 12
    immigrants, 95
    Kiwi, 12–13
    missionaries, 47–49
    pakeha, 90, *90*, 91
    polynesian, 11
    tribes, 89
    women, 95
Peters, Winston, 68
plant life, 12–13, 39–41, 81–82
    environmental concerns, 32
pohutukawa tree, 41
police officer, *70*
political parties, 68
population, 12, 20, 25, 26, 47, 54, 71,
    90, 93–95

Q

Queenstown, 125

R

rabbit, 36
radiata pine, 81–82, *82*

Rainbow Warrior, 59, *59*
red deer, *76*
religion, 97
    Christianity, 97–98, 99–100
    Godzone, 97
rimu tree, 41
Ring of Fire, 15, *22*
rivers and lakes, 19, 21
roadways, 120–122, *121*
Rutherford, Ernest, 56, *56*

S

scientific research, 85–86
seal hunters, 46
sealife, *38*, 38–39, *39*
sheep, 36, 54, 78, *79*, 79–80
sheepdogs, 79, *79*
shrunken heads, 46, *47*
skateboards, 120
Snell, Peter, 106
social reforms, 58
Southern Alps, 15–16, 22–24, *24*, 26
South Island, *15*, 18, *18*, 22–26
sports, 87, 105–107
    bungee jumping, 9, *9*, 13, 125

mountaineering, 24
rugby, 104, *104*
skiing, *24*
white water rafting, 19, *19*
yacht racing, 108–109, *109*
students, *119*
sunrise, 20
Sutherland Falls, 28, *29*

T

Tait, Blyth, 107
takahe bird, *31*, 33
Tasman, Abel, *44*, 44–45
Tasman Glacier, *24*
tattoos, 111, *111*
Te Atairangikaahu, Queen, 64, *64*
tectonic plates, 15
Te Marae, *100*, 100–101, *101*
Te Papa Museum, 89, 115
Te Wahipounamu, 26, 27
Thompson, William, 52
thumbprints, 89
timeline, historic, 128–129
Todd, Mark, 107
Tongariro National Park, 26, *26*, 27

tourism, 13, 58, 81, 86–87
trade, 46–47, 53, 54–55, 58, 61
traffic, 120–122, *121*
transportation, 54–55, 120–122, *121*
traveling, 120
Treaty of Waitangi, 49, 50, 51, 63–64
tuatara lizard, 34, *34*
Tunzelmann, Alexander von, 85
Tuwharetoa, Ngati, 27

U

University of Otago, *124*, 125

V

village cottage, *13*
vineyards, *74*, 82
volcanoes, 15, 21, 22
voting rights, 66

W

Waitangi Day, 65
Waitangi Treaty House, *62*
Walker, John, 106

war dance (haka), 103, *103*
waterfalls, 28
weights and measures, 86
Wellington, 73, 123
Westland, 22
weta (insect), 35, *35*
whale hunters, 46
whales, 38
Wherowhero, Te, 52
wildlife, 87
    birds, 12, *12, 30, 31, 31–34, 33*
    conservation, *32–33*
    endangered/extinct, *32–33,* 59
    environmental concerns, 32
    glowworms, 37
    insects, 34, 35
    non-native species, 32, 36
    reserves, *32–33*
    sealife, *38,* 38–39, *39*
    sheep, 36
wine industry, 82
wood carving, *110*
Woods, John Joseph, 72
World Heritage Sites, 26–27
World War I, 55–56
World War II, 57

Meet the Author

DONNA WALSH SHEPHERD's first trip to New Zealand came quite by accident. She was heading to a wedding in Australia when the plane stopped in New Zealand to refuel. When it was delayed, she was able to extend the stopover for a few days of visiting North Island. It reminded her very much of western Washington, where she grew up. Since then she has met many people who say, "You're writing about New Zealand; I love New Zealand! It reminds me so much of . . ." Then they add California or Colorado or Japan or Alaska or England or New England or somewhere else that makes them smile. She thinks New Zealand must remind people of beautiful places where they feel welcome and at home.

To do the research for this book, she began by reading and talking to people. She set up her computer to receive the New Zealand morning headline news and weekly government reports. "But," she says, "you can't write a book by only reading other books and Web sites. Visiting a place changes everything. Suddenly, the odd string of letters you can't pronounce becomes a real place full of kind people and beautiful vistas." As she began to arrange her research trip, everyone who found

out wanted to go. "I could have easily had 200 traveling companions had I let everyone who wanted to, come along."

The challenge in writing about a subject as broad and diverse as New Zealand is how to fit in as much as possible. Almost always, as she writes and researches, she finds herself being quite amazed by her topic, no matter what it is. That was certainly the case with New Zealand. A few of her surprises while in New Zealand—how wonderful the food was; how long it took to drive anywhere, yet how empty the roads were; how pleasant and easygoing the people were. And how much it could rain! She spent six days in Queenstown when the worst flood in 150 years washed out all roads.

When not writing about wonderful places like New Zealand, Donna Walsh Shepherd lives in Alaska and teaches writing at the University of Alaska.

Photo Credits

A Perfect Exposure: 64 bottom, 133 bottom (The Evening Post), 84, 132 bottom (Mike Clare)

AP/Wide World Photos: 107 (Will Burgess), 104 (Eduardo Di Baia), 21 (Allan Gibson/New Zealand Herald), 61 (Al Green/Royal Australian Air Force), 68 (Dave Hallett), 11 (Ross Setford), 69 (Ross Setford/Fotopress), 109 (Jack Smith), 64 top (John Stillwell, PA), 95 (Phil Walter/Fotopress), 108

Art Resource, NY/Werner Forman/National Museum of New Zealand, Wellington, New Zealand: 33 top

Auscape: 106 (Andy Belcher), 16, 101 (Jean-Paul Ferrero), 2 (Nick Groves/Hedgehog House), 9 (Steven David Miller), 76, 124 (Colin Monteath)

BBC Natural History Unit: 91 top, 133 top (John Cancalosi), 26 (Jeremy Walker)

Bill Bachman & Associates: 23, 24, 87 top, 90 top, 131 bottom

Bob and Suzanne Clemenz: 83, 99

Corbis-Bettmann: 20 (AFP), 59, 77, 114 (Kevin Fleming), 57 (Hulton-Deutsch), 36 (Peter Johnson), 123 (Craig Lovell), 63, 70, 71 top (Paul A. Souders), 62 (Nik Wheeler), 56 bottom

Dave G. Houser/HouserStock, Inc.: 74, 103

Dembinsky Photo Assoc./Richard Hamilton Smith: 8

Getty Images: 112 (George De Sota), 113 (Universal International Television), 115 (Chris Weeks)

International Stock Photo/Miwako Ikeda: 98

Mary Evans Picture Library: 42, 44, 45 bottom, 47, 51, 52, 53, 56 top

Minden Pictures: 12, 78 (Tui De Roy), 31 (Mitsuaki Iwago), 37, 38, 40 (Konrad Wothe)

Nik Wheeler: 13, 91 bottom, 122

Peter Arnold Inc.: 19 (Arlene Burns), 102 (John Cancalosi), 111 right (Robert C. Gildart), 82 (Walter H. Hodge)

Photo Researchers, NY: 33 bottom (Mark Boulton), 30 (Gregory G. Dimijian), 87 bottom, 119 top (John Eastcott/Yva Momatiuk), 35 (Brian Enting), 39 (David Hall), 34 (Tom McHugh)

Stone/Getty Images: 7 top, 96 (Chad Ehlers), 29 (David Hiser), 25, 130 left (Robert Knight)

Superstock, Inc.: 48 (A.K.G., Berlin), 15, 18, 41, 67, 93

The Image Works: cover, 6, 79, 81 (Eastcott), 105, 89 (John Eastcott/Yva Momatiuk)

Viesti Collection, Inc.: 7 bottom, 88, 111 left

Wolfgang Kaehler: 80, 86, 90 bottom, 94 left, 100, 126, 132 top

Woodfin Camp & Associates: 121, 117 (John Eastcott/Yva Momatiuk), 119 bottom (Adam Woolfitt), 14, 110, 116 (Mike Yamashita)

Maps by Joe LeMonnier